Mountain Interiors
Intérieurs des montagnes

Beate Wedekind

Edited by | Herausgegeben von | Sous la direction de
Angelika Taschen

Mountain Interiors
Intérieurs des montagnes

TASCHEN

KÖLN LONDON LOS ANGELES MADRID PARIS TOKYO

Umschlagvorderseite | Front cover | Couverture:
Gästezimmer im Haus »Casanna« von Rudolf Haene
Guest room in Rudolf Haene's house "Casanna"
Chambre d'amis dans la maison «Casanna» de Rudolf Haene
Photo: Reto Guntli

Umschlagrückseite | Back cover | Dos de couverture &
Abbildung S. 30/31 | Reproduction page 30/31 | Illustration page 30/31:
Beim Col du Tricot, in der Nähe des Mont Blanc, Savoyen
Close to the Col du Tricot, near Mont Blanc, Savoie
Le Col du Tricot à proximité du Mont-Blanc, Savoie
Photo: Galen Rowell/Franca Speranza

Abbildung Seite 2 | Reproduction page 2 | Illustration page 2:
Kuckucksuhr, La Ferme d'Hauteluce
Cuckoo clock, La Ferme d'Hauteluce
Un coucou, La Ferme d'Hauteluce
Photo: Giorgio Possenti/Vega MG

Abbildung Seite 7 | Reproduction page 7 | Illustration page 7:
Edelweiß *(Leontopodium alpinum)*
Photo: Richard Müller

Die Photos der Einleitung stammen aus folgenden Büchern:
The photos from the introduction were taken from the following books:
Les photos de l'introduction sont extraites des livres suivants:
Die Alpen. Herausgegeben von Hans Schmithals. Ernst Wasmuth AG, Berlin 1926
Karl Springenschmid, *Bauern in den Bergen.* Fotos von Peter Paul Atzwanger,
   Wegweiser-Verlag GmbH Berlin, F. Bruckmann Verlag KG, 1936
Luis Trenker, *Berge im Schnee. Das Winterbuch,* Th. Knaur Nachf. Verlag, Berlin 1935
Luis Trenker und Walter Schmidkunz, *Berge und Heimat. Das Buch von den Bergen
   und ihren Menschen,* Th. Knaur Nachf. Verlag, Berlin 1933

Abbildung S. 254/255 | Reproduction page 254/255 | Illustration page 254/255:
Ansicht des Weilers Noversch im Tal von Gressoney, Aostatal
View of the hamlet of Noversch in the Gressoney Valley, Valle d'Aosta
Le hameau de Noversch dans la vallée de Gressoney, Val d'Aoste
Photo: Robert Tixador/Agence TOP

© 2003 TASCHEN GmbH
Hohenzollernring 53, D–50672 Köln
www.taschen.com

Original edition © 1998 Benedikt Taschen Verlag GmbH
© 2002 VG Bild-Kunst, Bonn, for the works by Christian Ludwig Attersee,
Balthus Klossowski de Rola, Sandro Chia, Alberto Giacometti, Sonja Knapp,
Henri Laurens, Anne and Patrick Poirier, Setsuko
© 2002 The Andy Warhol Foundation, New York, for the works by Andy Warhol
Edited and designed by Angelika Taschen, Cologne
Cover design: Angelika Taschen, Cologne
Research, selection and texts by Beate Wedekind, San Mateo/New York
Text edited by Ursula Fethke, Cologne
Production: Ute Wachendorf, Cologne
English translation by Isabel Varea, London
French translation by Annie Berthold, Düsseldorf
Picture research: Oda Schäfer, Hamburg, Ursula Fethke, Cologne
Coordination: Pluis Mulder, San Rafael

Printed in Italy
ISBN 3-8228-2390-2

Inhalt
Contents
Sommaire

Wohnen, wo die Götter hausen
Von Beate Wedekind

Living in the Home of the Gods
By Beate Wedekind

Vivre dans la demeure des dieux
De Beate Wedekind

Reinhold Messner, Bergsteiger, Dokumentar-Filmer, Autor und Umweltschützer, lebt auf seiner Burg Juval hoch über dem Südtiroler Schnalstal. In der Burgkapelle, die das Ende eines langen Flurs bildet, hat er seine Sammlung zur 3 000 Jahre währenden Geschichte hinduistischer, buddhistischer und christlicher Religion ausgestellt. In einem anderen Stockwerk befindet sich Messners »Yeti-Höhle«. Hier zeigt er Fotos und Zeugnisse der frühen Bergmenschen, deren Spuren er ausfindig gemacht hat. Manche Leute verweisen allerdings Messners Forschung in die Fabelwelt. Der Bergsteiger nimmt es gelassen. Er ist wie kein anderer Mensch herumgekommen auf den Höhen der Welt: Alle Achttausender des Himalaja hat er bezwungen – und das ohne Atemgerät und mit klarem Verstand.

Schon immer rankten sich die wundersamsten Sagen um Berggeister und -götter. »Schimmernde Krone der Welt, ihre Häupter glänzen weithin in der Sonne. Wie Symbole der Ewigkeit erheben sie sich in die Unendlichkeit des Himmels«, schrieb Luis Trenker, der, ein Landsmann Messners, wie dieser der Bergwelt verfallen war. In der indischen Sage heißt es, daß Gott die Berge aus geflügelten Wolken erschuf. Die Muslime glauben, daß der Schaum der gebärenden Wogen der Weltmeere sich zu den festen Gebirgen der Kontinente formte. Die höchsten Gipfel der bolivianischen Anden sollen die steingewordenen Häupter zweier Riesen sein, die sich im Urkampf gegenseitig abgeschlagen haben.

Am liebsten ist mir die ungarische Legende, die seit Generationen so erzählt wird: Als die irdischen Tage Christi gezählt waren und der Gottessohn gen Himmel fuhr, wollte sich die Erde nicht von ihm trennen. Und so folgten ihm die Steine, der Sand, der Fels und der Boden, bis Gott ihnen Einhalt gebot. Unter dem Abschiedssegen Christi erstarrten die zu Bergen gewordenen Jünger in der Höhe, die sie auf ihrem Weg zum Himmel erreicht hatten.

Wie Goethe die Berge entdeckte
In Reisehandbüchern aus der Mitte des 18. Jahrhunderts werden die Berge als »schröcklich und grausam hoch« beschrieben. Von der Schönheit der Natur ist keine Rede, denn um diese zu entdecken, hätte man

Bei Saas-Fee gegen das Allalinhorn, Wallis
Near Saas-Fee, with the mountain
Allalinhorn in the background, Valais
La montagne d'Allalinhorn vue des environs de
Saas-Fee, Valais
Photo: Jean Gaberell

At his Juval Fortress high above South Tyrol's Schnals Valley, in a chapel leading off a long corridor, Reinhold Messner, mountaineer, film-maker, author and environmentalist, has assembled a collection symbolising 3 000 years of world religions – Hinduism, Buddhism and Christianity. On another floor, Messner has created a "Yeti's Cave", in which he displays photographs and other evidence of early mountain people, whose traces he has himself discovered. Some people consign Messner's research to the realms of fantasy. Messner is unperturbed. He, like no other, has seen the world's mountaintops, having conquered all the Himalayan summits over 8 000 metres, without breathing apparatus and with all his wits about him.

Many marvellous myths have been woven around the gods and spirits of the mountains. "Shimmering pinnacles of the world, their peaks gleaming for miles around in the sunlight. Like symbols of eternity, they rise into the infinity of the heavens", wrote Luis Trenker who, like his compatriot Messner, became addicted to the mountains. An Indian legend tells how God created the mountains from winged clouds. Muslims believe that the foam of waves of the world's oceans fossilised to form the rocky mountain ranges of the Asian continent. According to a story told by native tribes, the highest mountains in the Bolivian Andes are the heads of feuding giants killed in battle and now turned to stone.

My favourite is the Hungarian legend, handed down through succeeding generations. When Christ's days on earth were numbered and God was leading Him heavenwards, the Earth did not want to be separated from Him. And so stones, rocks, sand and soil continued to follow Him, until God commanded them to go no further. After receiving a divine farewell blessing, these earthly disciples were transformed into mountains at the height they had reached on the pathway to Heaven.

How Goethe discovered the mountains
Guidebooks available to 18th-century travellers described the mountains as "terrible and dreadfully high", making no mention at all of the beauty of the landscape. In order to explore, visitors would have

Dans la chapelle située au débouché d'un long corridor de son château de Juval, qui surplombe la vallée de Schnalstal, dans le Tyrol du Sud, Reinhold Messner, alpiniste, auteur de films, écrivain, écologiste, présente 3 000 ans de symbolique hindouiste, bouddhique et chrétienne. A un autre étage, il a aménagé une «grotte du yéti» où sont exposés des photos et des témoignages de l'existence de «l'abominable homme des neiges». Certains tiennent les recherches de Messner pour une galéjade et une chimère, mais lui n'en a cure. Personne n'a autant couru les sommets du monde et ne peut afficher à son palmarès l'intégralité des 8 000 mètres himalayens qu'il a conquis sans oxygène et l'esprit clair.

Depuis la nuit des temps, les plus belles légendes se sont tissées autour des génies et des dieux de la montagne. «Coupole étincelante du monde, tes sommets continuent de miroiter au soleil et se dressent dans l'infini des cieux tels des symboles de l'éternité», écrit Luis Trenker, un compatriote de Messner, tombé lui aussi sous le charme de la montagne.

Selon une vieille croyance de l'Inde, Dieu aurait créé les montagnes avec des nuages ailés. Pour les musulmans, elles sont nées de l'écume lapidifiée des océans. D'après une légende indienne, les plus hauts sommets des Andes boliviennes sont les têtes pétrifiées de deux géants qui se seraient décapités l'un l'autre au cours d'un formidable combat primordial.

Mais l'histoire que je préfère est originaire de Hongrie: lorsque les jours de Jésus furent comptés et qu'il commença son ascension vers le ciel, la terre ne voulut en aucun cas se séparer de lui. Les pierres, le sable, la roche et le sol le suivirent jusqu'à ce que Dieu les arrêtât. Le Christ leur fit alors ses adieux et sous sa bénédiction céleste, ces éléments se figèrent en montagnes à la hauteur qu'ils avaient atteinte en l'accompagnant vers le firmament.

Comment Goethe découvrit la montagne
Les récits de voyage du 18e siècle décrivent les montagnes comme «effrayantes et affreusement hautes». Aucune allusion à la beauté de la nature. Car, si les montagnes se découvrent à pied, à l'époque, il n'était pas question de randonner. On se déplaçait sur des

Der Alte aus dem Sarntal, Südtirol
An old man from the Sarentina Valley, South Tyrol
Vieux montagnard de la Sarentine, Tyrol du Sud
Photo: Peter Paul Atzwanger

Das Matterhorn, Wallis
The Matterhorn, Valais
Le Cervin, Valais
Photo: Georg Neumann

Gletschertisch in den Ötztaler Alpen, Tirol
Glacial shelf in the Ötztal Alps, Tyrol
Table de glacier, massif de l'Ötztal, Tyrol
Photo: Richard Müller

wandern müssen. Und Zufußgehen war damals keineswegs angesehen. Statt dessen ließ man sich von Tragtieren hinaufbefördern und war stolz, wenn man auf diese bequeme Art und Weise Aussichtspunkte in 1 500 oder gar 2 000 Meter Höhe bezwang.

Auch Johann Wolfgang von Goethe konnte bei seiner ersten Reise in die Schweizer Berge 1775 mit der Schönheit der Landschaft nur wenig anfangen. Er fühlte sich »verwirrt und beunruhigt« und war nicht einmal in der Lage, das Gesehene in einer Zeichnung festzuhalten, was er sonst auf seinen Reisen immer tat. Vier Jahre später bestieg Goethe von Chamonix aus mit Herzog Karl August von Weimar den Col de Balme und wanderte weiter durch das tiefverschneite Rhonetal zu den Pässen Furka und St. Gotthard. Nun war der Bann gebrochen, Goethe liebte die Berge. Glücklich schrieb er an Charlotte von Stein: »... der Knoten, der uns den Weg verstrickte, ist entzweigeschnitten«. Als er später auf seiner italienischen Reise die bayerischen Berge sah, erschloß sich ihm »eine neue Welt«.

Bald befiel Goethe ein großer Wissensdurst, und er zeichnete alles: Pflanzen, Tiere und Gestein. Nicht genug damit: In seinem wissenschaftlichen Forschungsdrang klopfte er auf dem Gotthard sorgfältig und fleißig Steine und nahm sie säckeweise mit nach Hause. Im Goethe-Haus zu Weimar kann man einige davon noch heute bewundern. Sogar ein Edelweiß soll Goethe gepflückt haben. Umweltschutz war damals noch nicht opportun.

Die Madonna von St. Moritz

Das Badrutt Palace ist ein Fünf-Sterne-Hotel und Synonym für den märchenhaften Aufstieg von St. Moritz vom bitterarmen Engadiner Bergdorf zum berühmtesten Wintersportort der Welt. Der Gastwirt Johannes Badrutt, ein Ahn des heutigen Hoteliers, begründete 1864 den Ruhm des Ortes mit einer Wette. Vier englischen Sommergästen versprach er freie Logis und Kost sowie die Erstattung der Reisekosten von London nach St. Moritz, wenn sie im Winter wiederkämen. Sie kamen zu Weihnachten mit dem Pferdeschlitten über den Julierpaß – halbblind, weil sie ihre Sonnenbrillen vergessen hatten – und blieben bis Ostern.

been obliged to walk – and this was simply not the done thing at the time. So they resorted to horseback and were proud when, using this more comfortable means of transport, they reached vantage points at altitudes of 1 500 or even 2 000 metres.

Even Johann Wolfgang von Goethe, on his first visit to the Swiss Alps in 1775, felt "bewildered and ill at ease", and was not even capable of making sketches of what he had seen, as he always did when travelling. Four years later, in the company of Prince Karl August of Weimar, he climbed from Chamonix to the Col de Balme and crossed the deep snows of the Rhône Valley and over the Furka and St. Gotthard Passes. The spell was broken, Goethe fell in love with the mountains. Gleefully, he wrote to his close friend Charlotte von Stein: "...the knot in which our path was entangled has been cut in twain." Later, on the way to Italy, he saw the Bavarian Alps, "a new world" opened up to him. Writing about the Brenner Pass he declared: "It becomes ever more beautiful, it is beyond description".

Soon Goethe's curiosity got the better of him. He sketched everything: plants, animals and rocks. As if that were not enough, in the interests of scientific research, he began carefully and diligently chipping away at the rocks and taking them home by the sackful. Some of these can still be seen at the Goethe House in Weimar. He is even reported to have picked an edelweiss. In those days environmental protection was not yet an issue.

The Madonna of St. Moritz

The Badrutt Palace is a five-star hotel which symbolises the legendary rise of St. Moritz from a desperately poor mountain village in the Engadine to the world's most renowned winter sports resort. It all began in 1864 with a wager made by innkeeper Johannes Badrutt, an ancestor of the present hotelier. He promised four summer visitors from England that he would provide them with free board and lodging, and pay for their journey from London to St. Moritz if they were to return in winter. They came at Christmas, in a horse-drawn sleigh over the Julier Pass – half-blinded because they had left their sunglasses behind – and stayed until Easter.

mules et on était fier d'atteindre d'une manière aussi agréable un beau point de vue à 1 500 ou même 2 000 mètres d'altitude.

Johann Wolfgang von Goethe n'échappe pas non plus à cette vision étriquée de l'univers montagneux. Lors de son premier voyage en Suisse, en 1775, il ne se montre guère sensible à la beauté du paysage. Il se sent «déconcerté et inquiet» et, contrairement à ses habitudes, n'est même pas capable de dessiner ce qu'il a vu. Quatre ans plus tard, depuis Chamonix, il monte au col de Balme en compagnie du duc Karl August de Weimar et poursuit son voyage à pied dans la vallée du Rhône enneigée, en passant par les cols de la Furka et du Saint-Gothard. Goethe tombe instantanément sous le charme. Heureux, il écrit à Charlotte de Stein: «... le nœud qui nous embrouillait le chemin s'est enfin brisé». Quelques années plus tard, au cours de son voyage en Italie, il découvre tout à coup «un monde nouveau» en apercevant les Alpes bavaroises. Il évoque le Brenner en ces termes: «C'est de plus en plus beau, aucun mot ne peut le décrire.»

Une curiosité fébrile s'empare bientôt de Goethe. Il dessine tout: les plantes, les animaux, les minéraux. Il va même plus loin: au Gothard, emporté dans son élan scientifique, il casse soigneusement des morceaux de roche et les ramène par sacs entiers. Dans la maison de Goethe à Weimar, on peut en voir encore quelques specimens, ainsi qu'un edelweiss qu'il avait lui-même cueilli (la protection de la nature était encore une notion inconnue!).

La Madone de Saint-Moritz

Rien ne symbolise mieux la fabuleuse métamorphose du pauvre village engadin qu'était Saint-Moritz en station de sports d'hiver la plus célèbre au monde, que le fameux Badrutt Palace, un hôtel cinq étoiles fondé en 1864 par l'aubergiste Johannes Badrutt, ancêtre de l'actuel hôtelier. Cette année-là, il scella le sort du petit village en faisant un pari avec quatre estivants britanniques: il leur promit de les accueillir gratuitement, et même de leur payer les frais du voyage depuis Londres, s'ils revenaient en hiver. Ils revinrent en effet, en traîneau tiré par des chevaux, par le col de Julier, à moitié aveugles (ils avaient oublié leurs lunettes de soleil), et restèrent jusqu'à Pâques.

Partnachklamm im Winter, Garmisch
Winter in the Partnachklamm gorge, Garmisch
Les gorges du Partnachklamm en hiver, Garmisch
Photo: Hans Huber

Hochkrumbach, Bregenzerwald
Village of Hochkrumbach, Bregenzerwald
region
Hameau de Hochkrumbach, la forêt de
Bregenz
Photo: Hugo Mylius

Berghütte Einödsbach gegen die Trettachspitze und Mädelegabelgruppe, Allgäu
The mountain refuge of Einödsbach
set against the Trettachspitze and the Mädelegabel mountain range, Allgäu region
Chalet d'Einödsbach au pied du Trettachspitze
et du massif du Mädelegabel, Allgäu
Photo: Alfred Asal

Warscheneckgruppe mit Hofalmhütte,
Salzkammergut
Warscheneck mountain range with alpine hut,
Salzkammergut region
Chalet d'alpage dans le massif du
Warscheneck, Salzkammergut
Photo: Konrad Heller

Großer Reichenstein, Sparafeld und Kalbling
mit Mödlinger Hütte, Oberösterreich
Mödlinger mountain hut set against the
mountains of Großer Reichenstein, Sparafeld
and Kalbling, Upper Austria
Le Grand Reichenstein, le Sparafeld et le
Kalbling, avec un chalet typique de Mödling,
Haute-Autriche
Photo: Erwin Hilscher

Alpen Interieurs   Einleitung

Innergschlöß gegen Venedigergruppe, Tirol
Village of Innergschlöß set against the
Venediger mountain range, Tyrol
Hameau d'Innergschlöß dans le massif du
Venediger, Tyrol
Photo: Otto Schob

An der Route zum Großen Sankt Bernhard bei
Liddes, Wallis
Near Liddes on the road to the Great
St. Bernard Pass, Valais
Sur la route du Grand-Saint-Bernard, près de
Liddes, Valais
Photo: Jean Gaberell

Sisikon am Vierwaldstätter See gegen den
Uri-Rotstock
Sisikon on Lake Lucerne with the Uri-Rotstock
in the background
Village de Sisikon au bord du lac des Quatre-
Cantons, au pied du massif du Rotstock,
canton d'Uri
Photo: Jean Gaberell

Die Glières vom Col de la Vanoise, Savoyen
The Glières from Col de la Vanoise, Savoie
Les Glières depuis le col de la Vanoise, Savoie
Photo: Otto Rögner

Alte Frau mit Schafen, Graubünden
Old woman with sheep, Grisons
Vieille bergère avec son troupeau de moutons, Grisons
Photo: I. Feuerstein

Die jungen Russen, die heute sommers wie winters Garantie für den Boom von St. Moritz sind, tragen ihre Sonnenbrillen Tag und Nacht. Ihr Wintersport ist allerdings meist das Nachtleben – und das Luxus-Shopping. Sie zahlen bar, in der Regel in Dollar, und ihre Frauen sind schön und unersättlich.

Neulich stand ich in der Halle des Badrutt in der Nähe des goldgerahmten Gemäldes »Mariä Himmelfahrt«. In Hörweite versuchte gerade eine italienische Gräfin, deren Familie schon in der dritten Generation nach St. Moritz kommt und die eine Kunsthistorikerin von Format ist, einem jungen Russen zu erklären, daß dieses Gemälde dem großen Raffael zugeschrieben wird. »Wieviel?« fragte der Russe und zog ein Bündel 1 000-Dollarscheine aus seiner Hosentasche. Die Italienerin lachte nicht.

Hansi Berger, Johann Sebastian Bach und Frau Flicks Kuh

Wenn man von Oberaudorf im Chiemgau die Straße hinauf in Richtung Tatzelwurm nimmt, kommt man irgendwann nach Seebach, einem Weiler von fünf Gehöften. Hier leben seit einigen Generationen die Bergers. Der älteste Hof wurde Anfang des 17. Jahrhunderts gebaut, der jüngste 1988. Das alte wie das neue Gebäude bestehen aus Fichtenholz, das in den eigenen Wäldern geschlagen wurde. Die Haustür des zweiten Hofs auf der linken Straßenseite steht offen und heraus tanzen wundersame Töne.

Der elfjährige Hansi Berger sitzt an der Orgel in der Diele und spielt eine Fuge von Johann Sebastian Bach. Er spielt ohne Noten, einfach so, mit Verve, Liebe und kindlicher Freude. Hansi und sein Vater verehren den großen Komponisten wie keinen anderen und wollen ihn in den nächsten Tagen mit einem fulminanten Hauskonzert feiern.

Hansi hat das absolute Gehör, und er braucht nur ein Musikstück zu hören, schon kann er es spielen, auf dem Klavier, auf der Zither oder auf der Orgel. Genauso wie sein Vater Hans, der studierter Kirchenmusiker ist und aus Liebe zur Musik als junger Mann auf den Erbhof verzichtete. Hans Berger hat eisblaue Augen, die tausend kleine Fältchen rahmen, denn erstens lacht er gerne und zweitens trägt er nie eine Sonnenbrille.

The young Russians, who now ensure that St. Moritz continues to prosper in both summer and winter, wear their sunglasses day and night. For them, winter sport usually means nightlife – and shopping for luxury goods. They pay in cash, usually in dollars, and their womenfolk are good-looking and insatiable.

Recently, I was standing in the lobby of the Badrutt, near the painting of "The Assumption of the Madonna" in its gilded frame. Within earshot, an Italian countess, an eminent art historian whose family has been coming to St. Moritz for three generations, was trying to explain to a young Russian that the painting was attributed to the great artist, Raphael. "How much?", asked the Russian, dipping into his trouser pocket and extracting a bundle of 1 000-dollar bills. The countess was not amused.

Hansi Berger, Johann Sebastian Bach and Frau Flick's cow

If you take the road from Oberaudorf in the Chiemgau up towards the Tatzelwurm, you eventually come across Seebach, a hamlet consisting of five farmhouses. The Bergers have lived here for several generations. The first of the farmhouses was built in the early 17th century, the most recent in 1988. Old and new alike are constructed from spruce wood, cut from trees in the family's own forests. The front door of the second house on the left-hand side of the road stands open; glorious sounds pour forth.

Eleven-year-old Hansi Berger is seated at the organ in the hall, playing a fugue by Johann Sebastian Bach. He plays from memory, with verve, love and a childish joy. Hansi and his father revere the great composer above all others, and will be honouring him with a dazzling concert at home in the next few days.

Hansi only needs to hear a piece of music and then he can play it, on the piano, zither or organ. Just like his father Hans, a formally trained church musician who gave up his inheritance for the sake of music, signing over the farm to his younger brother. Hans Berger is a man with ice-blue eyes, framed by a myriad of fine wrinkles, firstly because he laughs a great deal and secondly because he never wears sunglasses.

Aujourd'hui, les jeunes Russes qui, été comme hiver, assurent la prospérité de Saint-Moritz, ne quittent leurs lunettes de soleil ni le jour ni la nuit, et leurs sports d'hiver préférés sont plutôt la vie nocturne et le shopping de luxe. Ils paient cash, généralement en dollars, et leurs femmes sont belles et insatiables.

Je me trouvais récemment dans le grand hall du Badrutt, à proximité de la «L' Assomption de la Sainte Vierge» au magnifique encadrement en or, et surpris une conversation entre clients. Une comtesse italienne, historienne de l'art avertie, dont la famille fréquente Saint-Moritz depuis trois générations, tentait d'expliquer à un jeune Russe que cette œuvre était probablement de Raphaël. «Combien?» demanda le Russe en extirpant une liasse de billets de 1 000 dollars de sa poche. L'Italienne, abasourdie, ne rit pas.

Kühe auf der Alm
Cows in alpine pastures
Vaches sur l'alpe
Photo: Hans Pfeifer

Hansi Berger, Jean-Sébastien Bach et la vache de madame Flick

Sur la route qui monte de Oberaudorf au Tatzelwurm, dans le Chiemgau, on passe forcément par un hameau de cinq fermes du nom de Seebach. C'est là que vit depuis des générations la famille Berger. La plus ancienne ferme du hameau date du début du 17e siècle, la plus récente, de 1988. Elles ont toutes été construites en bois de mélèze, abattu dans les forêts de la propriété. La porte d'entrée de la seconde maison, à gauche de la route, est ouverte, et des sons merveilleux s'en échappent. Assis devant l'orgue du vestibule, Hansi Berger, un garçon de onze ans, interprète une fugue de Jean-Sébastien Bach. Comme ça, sans partition, avec une verve musicale et un plaisir enfantin évidents. Hansi et son père vénèrent le grand compositeur plus que tout et ils vont le fêter dans les prochains jours par une brillante matinée musicale.

Hansi a l'oreille absolue. Il écoute de la musique et peut la jouer aussitôt au piano, à la cithare et à l'orgue. Il tient de son père Hans, un organiste et cithariste, qui par amour de la musique a légué son héritage à son frère cadet. Les yeux de Hans Berger sont d'un bleu très clair, avec mille ridules tout autour car il rit volontiers et ne porte jamais de lunettes de soleil.

Schafe am Fuße der Bellavista, Berninagruppe
Sheep at the foot of Bellavista in the Bernina Alps
Berger avec ses moutons avec, à l'arrière-plan, la Bellavista dans le massif de la Bernina
Photo: Albert Steiner

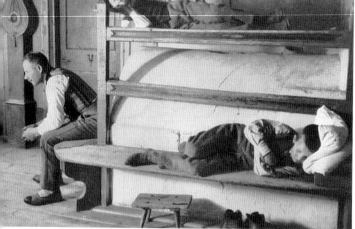

Ruheplatz am Ofen
A peaceful spot beside the stove
Coin repos près du poêle
Photo: Peter Paul Atzwanger

Mittagessen im Zillertal, Tirol
Lunchtime in the Ziller Valley, Tyrol
Repas de midi dans le Zillertal, Tyrol
Photo: Peter Paul Atzwanger

Beim Krapfenmachen in Hafling, Südtirol
Making "Krapfen" (carnival doughnuts) at
Avelengo, South Tyrol
Préparation des beignets de Carnaval
(«Krapfen») à Avelengo, Tyrol du Sud
Photo: Peter Paul Atzwanger

Rauchküche im Tuxertal, Tirol
Kitchen in the Tux Valley, Tyrol
Fumoir dans le Tuxertal, Tyrol
Photo: Peter Paul Atzwanger

Alpen Interieurs   Einleitung

Berghirte im Defereggental, Tirol
Mountain shepherd in the Defereggen Valley, Tyrol
Berger du Defereggental, Tyrol
Photo: Peter Paul Atzwanger

Schnitter im Inntal, Tirol
Cutting the crop in the Inn Valley, Tyrol
Faucheur de l'Inntal, Tyrol
Photo: Peter Paul Atzwanger

Rindermarkt im Eisacktal, Südtirol
Cattle market in the Eisack Valley, South Tyrol
Foire aux bestiaux dans la vallée de l'Isarco, Tyrol du Sud
Photo: Peter Paul Atzwanger

Erntetag
Harvest time
Jour de récolte
Photo: Peter Paul Atzwanger

Kinder am Werktag
Children on a working day
Enfants pendant une journée de travail
Photo: Peter Paul Atzwanger

Kleine Kinder aus dem Zillertal, Tirol
Small children from the Ziller Valley, Tyrol
Jeunes enfants du Zillertal, Tyrol
Photo: Peter Paul Atzwanger

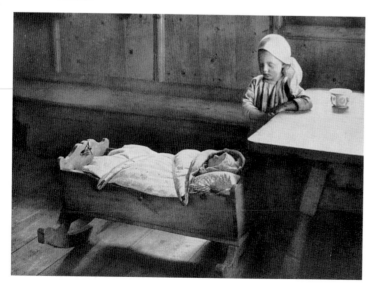

Berger spielt jeden Sonntag die Orgel unten in Oberaudorf; außerdem komponiert er und forscht nach
vergessener alpenländischer Musik. Nie würde er auf
die Idee kommen, aus Seebach wegzuziehen. Warum
auch: Gleich hinter den Bergen liegt Paris und dahinter das Meer. Manchmal unternimmt er einen Aus-
flug in die Welt. Dann fliegt er zum Beispiel mit seiner
Zither nach Argentinien, um in Buenos Aires ein Kon-
zert zu geben, und macht einen Abstecher auf die Ga-
lapagosinseln. Oder er spielt Dr. Friedrich Karl Flick,
dem reichsten Privatier Deutschlands, der Zithermu-
sik und besonders die von Hans Berger liebt, zum
Geburtstag auf.

So kommt es auch, daß im Stall der Bergers
eine Kuh steht, die Dr. Flicks Frau Ingrid gehört. Berger hatte bei einem Hauskonzert erzählt, daß eine
Kuh zum Schlachthof gebracht werden müsse. Das
verhinderte Frau Flick per Handschlag. Der Scheck
für den Kuhhandel kam postwendend. Die Kuh ist
mittlerweile eines natürlichen Todes gestorben, weshalb Frau Flick nun ein Kalb gehört.

Wider die bösen Geister

Gemütlich will man es haben, romantisch soll es
sein. Und so zog eines Tages der Country-Stil in Häuser und Wohnungen ein, bis in die modernsten Apartments der hektischsten Urbanisationen. Der Fleckerl-
teppich im Bad, das Steingutgeschirr in der Küche,
der blanke Holztisch im Eßzimmer, und als Erken-
nungszeichen für den ländlichen Geschmack hängt
über der Wohnungstür ein hübsch geflochtener Kranz.

Was ursprünglich ein alpenländischer Brauch
zur Abwehr von bösen Geistern und anderem Unheil
war, dient heute zwar als reines Dekorationselement,
erfüllt aber wahrscheinlich auch bei den Unwissen-
den dennoch seinen Zweck. Aus 77 heilbringenden
Kräutern, die man selbst in den Wäldern und Wiesen
der Gegend pflückte, flocht man einen Kranz, ließ ihn
an Mariä Himmelfahrt vom Priester segnen und
hängte ihn über die Tür.

In einigen Regionen der Alpen, vor allem im
bayerischen Oberinntal, wird auch heute noch nach
dem Almabtrieb der Kopfschmuck der Kuh, die wegen ihrer überragenden Milchleistung während des
Sommers besonders festlich geschmückt worden

Every Sunday, Berger plays the organ down in the village of Oberaudorf. He also composes and researches forgotten Alpine folk music. He would never dream of moving away from Seebach. Why should he? Paris is just over the mountains and then you come to the sea, and sometimes he ventures into the wider world. For example, he flies with his zither to Argentina to give a concert in Buenos Aires, and then makes a detour to the Galapagos Islands. Or he plays at the birthday celebrations of Dr. Friedrich Karl Flick, Germany's richest man of independent means, who loves zither music, especially that of Hans Berger.

This explains why, in the Bergers' cow shed, there is a cow belonging to Dr. Flick's wife Ingrid. At a private concert, Berger mentioned that a cow was due to be sent for slaughter. Frau Flick agreed to buy the cow, saving it's life. The cheque arrived with the very next post. The cow has since died from natural causes, which is why Frau Flick now owns a calf.

Against evil spirits

We like our homes to be cosy, we want our surroundings to be romantic. So, one day, rustic style found its way into houses and flats, even into state-of-the-art apartments in the most frantic of cities. The rag rug in the bathroom, the stoneware pots in the kitchen, the scrubbed wooden table in the dining room, and, to symbolise our countrified tastes, a pretty, plaited wreath over the front door.

What was once an Alpine custom to defend the home from evil spirits and other malign forces has become a purely decorative feature, which perhaps to some degree, albeit unacknowledged, fulfils its original purpose. In the old days, mountain-dwellers went to the woods to gather a cocktail of healing herbs to make their own wreaths. On the Feast of the Assumption, they had their wreath blessed by the local priest and hung it above the door.

Even today, in some Alpine regions, especially in Bavaria's Upper Inn Valley, the cow which yields the most milk over the season is garlanded with a festive headdress. After the herds are brought down from their summer pastures, this is hung on the wall

Berger joue tous les dimanches à l'orgue de Oberaudorf, compose et effectue des recherches sur la musique ancienne des Alpes. Il ne lui viendrait jamais à l'idée de quitter Seebach. Pourquoi le ferait-il d'ailleurs? Au-delà des montagnes, se trouvent Paris et, un peu plus loin, la mer. Parfois, il entreprend un voyage dans le monde. Il s'envole alors pour l'Argentine, avec sa cithare, pour donner un concert à Buenos Aires, et en profite pour faire un détour par les îles Galapagos. Ou bien il joue pour son ami Friedrich Karl Flick, le plus riche rentier d'Allemagne, à l'occasion de son anniversaire. Ce dernier est un amoureux de la musique pour cithare et particulièrement de celle de Hans Berger.

Voici comment l'étable des Berger héberge une vache qui appartient à madame Flick. A l'occasion d'un concert donné chez lui, Berger lui raconta qu'il fallait mener la bête à l'abattoir. Madame Flick s'y opposa et, à la manière des maquignons d'antan, topa dans la main de Berger. Le chèque, pour prix de la vente, arriva par la poste. La vache étant décédée entre-temps de mort naturelle, c'est maintenant un veau qui appartient à madame Flick.

Contre les esprits malfaisants

Confort accueillant et romantisme – telle est notre devise en matière d'habitat. Voilà pourquoi un jour le style «country» a pris possession des maisons et des demeures citadines, jusqu'aux appartements les plus modernes de nos centres urbains trépidants. Il est présent partout: tapis rustique en patchwork dans la salle de bains, service en grès dans la cuisine, table en bois nue dans la salle à manger, et surtout, insigne du goût champêtre en vogue, une jolie couronne d'herbes et de fleurs tressées est accrochée à la porte d'entrée. A l'origine, simple coutume alpine censée éloigner les esprits malfaisants et le mauvais œil, elle est devenue entre-temps un pur élément décoratif, ce qui ne l'empêche peut-être pas, d'ailleurs, à l'insu même de l'utilisateur ignorant, de remplir d'une manière ou d'une autre son rôle présumé. Composée de 77 herbes thérapeutiques cueillies dans les forêts et les alpages de la région, cette couronne était bénie par un prêtre le jour de l'Assomption puis accrochée à la porte de la maison.

Sarner Mädchen, Südtirol
Girl from the Sarentina Valley, South Tyrol
Jeune Sarentine, Tyrol du Sud
Photo: Peter Paul Atzwanger

Sarner Bursche, Südtirol
Boy from the Sarentina Valley, South Tyrol
Jeune Sarentin, Tyrol du Sud
Photo: Peter Paul Atzwanger

Pusterer Mädchen
Girl from the Puster Valley
Jeune fille du Pustertal
Photo: Peter Paul Atzwanger

war, an eine Wand im Stall oder über die Stalltür gehängt. Am Kranz baumeln Gerätschaften aus der Milchwirtschaft, Butterkübel, Kuhglocke und Milchgefäße, in Miniatur aus Holz geschnitzt. Das sieht hübsch aus und soll Wunder bewirken.

Das Schandmal der verlorenen Liebe

Diese Geschichte trug sich im Südtirol der zwanziger Jahre zu, aber sie könnte heute noch genauso passieren: Burgl und Luis waren einander versprochen. Ihre Familien lebten seit Generationen in demselben Dorf. Die beiden jungen Leute paßten gut zusammen. Beide waren fleißig, und sogar die Felder der Familien grenzten aneinander. Wenn Burgl einmal erbte, würde sich der Besitz von Luis vergrößern. Sie war also eine gute Partie. Mit Eifer und Ausdauer bearbeitete sie den Flachs. Jedes Jahr legte sie neue Bettwäsche und Tischwäsche in ihre Brauttruhe.

Dann plötzlich passierte es: Luis traf eine andere. Er hatte sie keineswegs gesucht, vielmehr war es Liebe auf den ersten Blick. Das aber durfte nicht sein. Als es beim zweiten und dritten Blick immer noch Liebe war und Luis seine Gefühle nicht mehr kontrollieren konnte, wurden seine Besuche bei Burgl immer seltener. Schließlich kam er gar nicht mehr. Luis, der Burgl nicht noch mehr verletzen wollte, beschloß, die andere in aller Stille in einem entfernten Wallfahrtsort zu heiraten. Im Dorf wußte man dennoch Bescheid, denn alle Neuigkeiten wurden von der Kanzel verkündet.

Am Hochzeitsmorgen fand man an Burgls Hausmauer unter dem Stubenfenster mit dicker Ölfarbe aufgemalt und weithin sichtbar ein giftgrünes Schandmal. »Reiter« nennt man in der Gegend die stilisierten Siebe, deren mittlere Löcher mit dicken Farbpunkten ausgemalt sind, den »Dorfaugen«. Burgl schämte sich und ging den Leuten wochenlang aus dem Weg. Sie blieb auf ihrer prall gefüllten Brauttruhe sitzen, die sie ganz hinten in die Kammer schob. So wie mit der Zeit ihre Liebe zu Luis verblaßte, verblaßte auch der grüne Reiter an der Hauswand.

»Wer den Schaden hat, braucht für den Spott nicht zu sorgen«, heißt es im Volksmund. Schandmale sind Zeichen von Schadenfreude, Neid, Boshaftigkeit und Spott, aber auch von Humor und Sympathie.

Drauntaler Mädchen
Girl from the Drava Valley
Jeune fille de la vallée de la Drave
Photo: Peter Paul Atzwanger

of the cow shed, or above the door, and from it dangle carved wooden miniatures of implements used in dairy farming, such as butter churns, cowbells and milk pails. It looks pretty and is also said to have miraculous powers.

The stigma of lost love

This is a tale from South Tyrol in the Twenties, but exactly the same thing could occur today: The story goes that Burgl and Luis were engaged. Their families had lived in the same village for generations. The young couple were well suited, both were hard workers and the two families' fields were even side by side. Once Burgl came into her inheritance, Luis's acreage would increase. They were a good match. With diligence and tenacity they grew and processed the flax crop. Each year Burgl added new bed and table linen to her bridal chest.

Then it happened: Luis met someone else. He could not help himself; it was not intentional, it was love at first sight. When that love endured on a second and third sighting and Luis could no longer control his feelings, he started to visit Burgl less and less often, until one day he stopped altogether. Luis, not wishing to cause Burgl any further pain, decided to marry the other girl quietly at a place of pilgrimage far away from the village. Even so, the village found out, for every piece of news was announced from the pulpit.

On the morning of the wedding, on the wall of Burgl's house, under the living room window, the eye of the village appeared, painted with thick oil paint in a bilious green. The stylised sieves, with a mesh in the middle daubed with thick splashes of paint, representing the eyes of the village, are known as "Reiter".

Mortified, Burgl hid away for weeks on end. She just sat on her amply filled bridal chest, which she had pushed away into a corner of the bedroom. As her love for Luis faded with time, so did the green "Reiter" on the wall.

Shameful stigmas such as this indicated delight in the misfortunes of others, envy, spite and ridicule, but also humour and understanding. As the old proverb says: "Don't mock the afflicted".

De nos jours encore, dans certaines régions des Alpes, dans le Oberinntal bavarois en particulier, on suspend à la fin de l'estivage la parure de la meilleure vache laitière sur un mur ou à la porte de l'étable. La couronne est également décorée des ustensiles laitiers: baratte, clarine et bidons à lait en miniature sculptés dans le bois. L'effet est des plus jolis et, en plus, on prétend que cela produit des miracles.

Dictons et météorologie alpine

«Quand la nuit du jour de l'an est pure et claire, l'année sera prospère.»

Le 6 février, c'est la Sainte-Dorothée, patronne des jardiniers. Celle-ci ne leur facilite pourtant pas la tâche puisque, selon un vieux dicton de paysans, «il neige souvent à la Sainte-Dorothée.»

Le 12 mars, on fête la Saint-Grégoire, que les paysans attendent toujours avec scepticisme: «Vent à la Saint-Grégoire, vent 40 jours durant.»

Si le paysan sème ses pommes de terre le 23 avril, à la Saint-Georges, patron des paysans, la récolte sera abondante.

Dans la nuit de Walpurgis, le 1er mai, les sorcières se réunissent pour danser. Aussi fait-on claquer les fouets et sonner les cloches pour éloigner les esprits malfaisants. On cache aussi les balais pour empêcher les sorcières de s'en servir de montures.

Si à la Saint-Jean, le 24 juin, qui marque le solstice d'été, les vers luisants brillent d'un éclat particulier, le dicton assure que «temps serein et clair invite à la danse en plein air. Mais si le ver luisant s'est caché jusqu'alors et après encore, c'est le mauvais temps pour longtemps.»

Le 26 juillet, à la Sainte-Anne, il convient d'observer les fourmis: «Quand les fourmis sont à l'ouvrage à la Sainte-Anne, l'hiver sera rude.»

Le 15 août est le jour de l'Assomption, la plus grande fête en l'honneur de la Vierge célébrée par l'Eglise catholique: «La Vierge du 15 août, en automne, arrange ou dérange tout.»

La Saint-Michel, que l'on célèbre le 29 septembre, est considérée comme le dernier jour de l'été. La tête décorée de fleurs, le bétail est ramené des alpages. Mais gare à la pluie: «Saint-Michel mouillé, automne manqué».

Ein Haus in Hafling, Südtirol
A house in Avelengo, South Tyrol
Maison d'Avelengo, Tyrol du Sud
Photo: Peter Paul Atzwanger

Bei Klosters, Prättigau
Near Klosters, Prättigau region
Aux environs de Klosters, région de Prättigau
Photo: Albert Steiner

Ein Wanderer an der Heiterwand bei der
Namloser Wetterspitze, Tirol
Walking on the Heiterwand in the Namloser
Wetterspitze range, Tyrol
Randonneur regardant le Heiterwand depuis
le Namloser Wetterspitze, Tyrol
Photo: Hans Pfeifer

Am Campo Tencia, Tessin
At Campo Tencia, Ticino
Sur le Campo Tencia, Tessin
Photo: Jean Gaberell

Anstieg zum Ortler von der Payerhütte, Süd-
tirol, mit Blick auf die Ötztaler Alpen
Path to the Ortler from the Payer mountain
hut, South Tyrol, with view of the Ötztal Alps
Ascension du Ortler depuis le refuge de Payer,
Tyrol du Sud, avec le panorama du massif de
l'Ötztal
Photo: Erwin Hoferer

Blick von den Kreuzbergen gegen die
Alvierkette, Appenzeller Land
View from the Kreuzberg mountains to the
Alvier mountain range, Appenzeller Land
La chaîne de l'Alvier vue des montagnes de
Kreuzberg, région d'Appenzell
Photo: Jean Gaberell

Alpen Interieurs   Einleitung

Aufstieg zur Zugspitze, Bayern
Climbing the Zugspitze, Bavaria
Ascension de la Zugspitze, Bavière
Photo: Heiß & Liescher

Auf dem Heimweg mit Blick auf das
Tennengebirge, Tennengau
Heading home facing the Tennen
mountains, Tennengau region
Sur le chemin du retour, face au versant nord
du Tennengebirge, région de Tennengau
Photo: Franz Kopfschlaegl

Auf dem Weg zur Kirche im Tuxertal, Tirol
On the way to church in the Tux Valley, Tyrol
En route pour l'église dans le Tuxertal, Tyrol
Photo: Peter Paul Atzwanger

Der letzte Weg
The last journey
Cortège funèbre
Photo: E. Meerkämper

Dorfmusikanten im Sarntal, Südtirol
Village musicians in the Sarentina Valley,
South Tyrol
Orchestre villageois dans la vallée de la
Sarentine, Tyrol du Sud
Photo: Peter Paul Atzwanger

Alphornbläser
Alpine horn player
Joueur de corne des Alpes
Photo: Jean Gaberell

Ein kleiner Wetterbericht aus den Alpen

»Die Neujahrsnacht hell und klar, deutet auf ein reiches Jahr.« So lautet die Bauernregel für die erste Nacht des Jahres.

Am 6. Februar wird dann St. Dorothee gefeiert, die Schutzpatronin der Gärtner, die es ihrer Berufsgruppe allerdings nicht leicht macht: »St. Dorothee bringt meistens Schnee« heißt es.

Am 12. März ist Gregorstag, den die Bauern immer skeptisch erwarten: »Weht am Gregoriustag der Wind, noch 40 Tage windig sind.«

Wenn der Bauer am 23. April, dem Namenstag des Heiligen Georg, dem Schutzpatron der Bauern, seine Kartoffeln setzt, bringen sie besonders reiche Ernte.

In der Nacht zum Walpurgistag, dem 1. Mai, tanzen die Hexen, weshalb um Mitternacht die Peitschen knallen und die Glocken läuten, um die bösen Geister zu verjagen. Die Hausfrauen verstecken vorher die Besen, damit die Hexen nicht auf ihnen reiten können.

Wenn am Johannistag, dem 24. Juni, Geburtstag Johannes' des Täufers und Tag der Sonnenwende, die Glühwürmchen besonders hell leuchten, sagt man: »Wenn die Johanniswürmchen schön leuchten und glänzen, kommt's Wetter zu Lust und im Freien zu Tänzen. Verbirgt sich das Tierchen bis Johanni und weiter, wird's Wetter einstweilen nicht warm und nicht heiter.«

Zu St. Anna am 26. Juli gilt es, die Ameisen zu beobachten: »Werfen die Ameisen an St. Anna auf, so folgt ein strenger Winter drauf.«

Mariä Himmelfahrt am 15. August ist das höchste Marienfest der katholischen Kirche. »Wie das Wetter an Mariäs Himmelfahrtstag, so der ganze Herbst sein mag.«

Der 29. September, der Tag des Erzengels Michael, gilt als letzter Sommertag. Das Vieh wird festlich geschmückt und von der Alm abgetrieben. Wehe, wenn es regnet: »Auf nassen Micheltag, nasser Herbst folgen mag.«

Gefürchtet ist der 28. Oktober, der Namenstag von Simon und Judas, denn die Bauernregel dazu lautet: »Simon und Juda, die zwei, führen oft Schnee herbei.«

A short Alpine weather forecast

"New Year's Eve is bright and clear, so we shall have a prosperous year." 6th February is the feast of St. Dorothy, patron saint of gardeners. According to Alpine farming lore, she does not make life easy for those she is supposed to protect: "St. Dorothy, snow we shall see."

Farmers await 12th March, St Gregory's Day, with some apprehension: "Blows the wind for Gregory, 40 days will windy be."

If seed potatoes are sown on 23rd April, the feast of St. George, patron saint of farmers, there will be an especially abundant crop.

Walpurgis Night, the eve of 1st May, is the witches' sabbath, which is why whips are cracked and bells rung at midnight to drive the evil spirits away. People also hide their brooms, to prevent the witches from riding on them.

The feast of St. John, 24th June, marks the birthday of John the Baptist and the summer solstice. According to tradition, much depends on whether glow-worms glow that night: "The worms on St John do glow and shine, we'll dance outside, for the weather is fine. If after St. John the wee beasties we see, the weather not bright nor warm will be."

On St. Ann's Day, 26th July, you have to keep an eye on the ants: "If ants on St. Ann's abound, harsh winter comes around."

The Feast of the Assumption on 15th August is the Catholic Church's most important celebration of the Virgin. "The rest of the autumn will be the same, as the weather we had when Assumption came."

Michaelmas, 29th September, is regarded as the last day of summer. Cattle are festively garlanded and brought down from the Alpine pastures. Woe betide the locals if it rains: "Michaelmas wet, damp autumn we'll get."

The feast of Simon and Jude, 28th October is anticipated with dread: "Simon and Jude, this pair, oft mean snow in the air."

The weather on St. Andrew's Day, 30th November, decides how it will turn out for the whole of the following year. "The weather on St. Andrew's Night may be cloudy, may be bright. Howe'er it be, we need not fear, 'twill be the same throughout the year."

Le 28 octobre est particulièrement redouté: «Saint-Simon et Saint-Jude, l'hiver est arrivé.»

Le 30 novembre, jour de la Saint-André, est fatidique pour le reste de l'année: «Pendant la nuit de la Saint-André, regarde le temps. Mauvais ou beau, il y est toute l'année.»

Vient enfin Noël: «Si le petit Jésus verse des larmes de pluie, ce sont quatre semaines sans soleil.»

Le chalet des Alpes

Pour survivre dans les montagnes, il fallait avoir un toit au-dessus de la tête. A l'origine, hommes et bêtes se partageaient un simple abri: l'étable. Cette habitation primitive était construite en grumes massives équarries et solidement jointes au moyen d'entailles.

Le toit d'un chalet typique est fait de planches de bois fendues à la main ou de bardeaux. On le parsème de grosses pierres pour le protéger du vent et des intempéries. Les pignons, toujours orientés vers le levant, regardent la vallée. Les faces exposées aux intempéries sont revêtues de bois, ce qui explique l'impression triste et sombre que font certains chalets lorsqu'on s'en approche du côté ouest. Mais en arrivant par l'est, la maison apparaît bien différente. Les murs exposés au soleil sont blanchis à la chaux, décorés de motifs aux couleurs vives et agrémentés de pignons, d'encorbellements et de balcons.

Les décors muraux extérieurs, peints dans des tons éclatants, sont souvent pleins d'entrain, un rien baroques. Les motifs sont généralement religieux: la Vierge Marie, la sainte Trinité, les saints de la maison – Florian, Léonard, Georges, Sébastien ou le géant Christophe. Sur les chalets sont inscrits des adages, pleins d'esprit et drôles pour la plupart. En voici un aperçu: «Construire une maison pourrait être un plaisir précieux. Je ne savais pas que c'était si ruineux», ou bien «Que Dieu protège les habitants de cette maison, même ceux qui y entrent et en sortent, et que seuls l'huissier et le percepteur, Il les éloigne de cette porte.»

Sarner Bauer, Südtirol
Farmer from the Sarentina Valley, South Tyrol
Paysan sarentin, Tyrol du Sud
Photo: Peter Paul Atzwanger

Skiparadies von Arosa, Graubünden
Arosa, Grisons, a paradise for skiers
Paradis pour skieurs dans la vallée d'Arosa,
Grisons
Photo: Albert Steiner

Im Sonntagsstaat
All dressed up
Parure de neige
Photo: I. Feuerstein

Eingeschneit
Snowed in
Paysage de toits enneigés
Photo: Risch-Lau

Skikjöring in Garmisch, Bayern
Skikjöring at Garmisch, Bavaria
Skikjöring à Garmisch, Bavière

Alpen Interieurs   Einleitung

Frühlingsboten
Harbingers of spring
Messagers du printemps
Photo: Jean Gaberell

Wintermärchen
Magical winter scene
Féerie hivernale
Photo: Albert Steiner

Spuren im Schnee
Tracks in the snow
Traces dans la neige
Photo: G. Brandt

Blick vom Bühlenhorn auf das Tinzenhorn und
Piz Michel, Graubünden
View of the Tinzenhorn and Piz Michel from
the Bühlenhorn, Grisons
Vue sur le Tinzenhorn et le Piz Michel depuis le
Bühlenhorn, Grisons
Photo: E. Meerkämper

Das Wetter des ganzen nächsten Jahres wird in der Nacht vom 30. November, dem Andreastag bestimmt: »Schau in der Andreasnacht, was für Gesicht das Wetter macht. So wie es ausschaut, glaub's fürwahr, bringt's gutes oder schlechtes Jahr.«

Schließlich gilt an Weihnachten: »Wenn Christkindlein Regen weint, vier Wochen keine Sonne scheint.«

Das Haus am Berg

Ohne Dach über dem Kopf gab es in den Bergen keine Existenz. Der Stall war der wichtigste Raum und die Wohnstube immer Teil des Stalls. Das ursprüngliche Alpenhaus wurde aus massiven vierkantigen Rundstämmen gebaut, die durch Kerben miteinander verfugt wurden. »Gestrickt« nennt man diese Bautechnik auch.

Das typische Dach eines Alpenhauses besteht aus handgespaltenen Brettern oder Schindeln, die zum Schutz gegen Wind und Wetter mit großen Steinen belegt sind. Die Hausgiebel sind immer der aufgehenden Sonne zugewandt und schauen ins Tal. Die Wetterseiten sind mit Holz verschalt. Deshalb wirken manche Häuser grau und trüb, wenn man sich ihnen von Westen her nähert. Kommt man dagegen von Osten, scheint es sich um ein anderes Haus zu handeln. Die Wände auf der Sonnenseite sind weiß getüncht, bunt bemalt, mit Giebeln, Erkern und Balkonen geschmückt.

Die farbige, oft schwungvolle, barocke Hausbemalung zeigt meistens religiöse Motive, die Muttergottes, die Heilige Dreifaltigkeit, die Hausheiligen Florian, Leonard, Georg, Sebastian oder den riesigen Heiligen Christopherus. Die Haussprüche haben oft einen verschmitzten Witz: »Das Häuser Bauen wäre eine Lust. Dass es so viel kost, hab ich nicht gewußt« oder »Gott schütze alle in diesem Haus, auch die da gehen ein und aus! Nur halt er fern von dieser Tür, den Steuerbot' und Gerichtsvollzieh'r.«

Finally comes Christmas. "If rainy tears from the Christ Child run, for four weeks more there will be no sun."

The house in the mountains

Without a roof over their heads people in the mountains simply could not survive. In the old days, the stable was the most important room under that roof, and the living quarters were part of the stable. These primitive houses were built of massive logs, cut square and fitted and held together by means of knotches – a building technique known as "stricken" (knitting).

Typically, the roof of an Alpine house is made with hand-chopped planks or shingles weighted down with heavy stones to protect it from wind and weather. The gables always face the rising sun and look down into the valley. The windward side is always wood-panelled, which is why many houses give a grey and gloomy impression when approached from the west. Viewed from the east, they look quite different. Walls facing the sun are whitewashed and brightly painted and adorned with gables, oriels and balconies.

The colourful, often opulent, baroque paintings on the houses are usually based on religious motifs: the Virgin Mary, the Holy Trinity, the local patron Saints Florian, Leonard, George or Sebastian, or enormous representations of St. Christopher. The inscriptions on the outer walls are often mischievously witty: "Building the house for me was a pleasure. The money it cost I repent at leisure", or "God preserve all those within, going out or coming in. Keep away from this, our door, the taxman and the force of law."

Kapelle von Eisten im Lötschental, Wallis
Chapel at Eisten, in the Lötschen Valley, Valais
Chapelle d'Eisten dans le Lötschental, Valais
Photo: Peter Paul Atzwanger

Whenever possible, Christian Ludwig Attersee likes to begin and end his day at the piano. He plays on a priceless Bösendorfer grand, in the music room of his house, the Villa Alber, to the east of Hotel Südbahn in the mountain resort of Semmering in the Austrian Alps. The house was built about 1890 and restructed about 1900 by the architect Franz von Neumann for the industrialist Leibenfrost and his family. Attersee is himself a synthesis of all the arts: painter, writer, musician, set-designer, performance artist, designer and art professor. He has represented his native Austria at such major artistic events as the documenta in Kassel and the Venice Biennale. He is a very busy man, but every Thursday evening he leaves Vienna for Semmering. The superb Villa Alber, perfectly maintained and magnificently furnished, is just one of his many different homes, a remarkable example of what he calls "Atterwelt" – "Atterworld".

Christian Ludwig Attersee

Der Tag von Christian Ludwig Attersee beginnt und endet – wenn es sich irgendwie einrichten läßt – am Klavier. Im Musikzimmer seiner Villa Alber, östlich vom Hotel Südbahn in der Villenkolonie am Semmering gelegen, spielt er an einem wertvollen Bösendorfer Flügel. Die Villa wurde um 1890 errichtet und um 1900 von dem Architekten Franz von Neumann für die Industriellenfamilie Leibenfrost umgebaut. Christian Ludwig Attersee ist ein Gesamtkunstwerk: Maler, Schriftsteller, Musiker, Bühnenbildner, Aktionskünstler, Designer und Kunstprofessor. Er vertrat sein Heimatland Österreich unter anderem bei der documenta in Kassel und auf der Biennale in Venedig. Jeden Donnerstagabend zieht es das Allround-Talent aus Wien hinaus an den Semmering. Die prachtvolle Villa Alber, perfekt erhalten und feudal ausgestattet, ist aber nur einer seiner sehr unterschiedlichen Wohnsitze – ein außergewöhnliches Beispiel für das, was er »Atterwelt« nennt.

La journée de Christian Ludwig Attersee – à condition, bien entendu, que son emploi du temps le lui permette – commence et s'achève au piano. Il possède un piano à queue Bösendorfer de grande valeur qu'il a installé dans la salle de musique de sa villa Alber, construite à l'est de l'hôtel Südbahn au col du Semmering, dans les Alpes autrichiennes, et restructurée par l'architecte Franz von Neumann vers 1900 pour une famille d'industriels, les Leibenfrost. Christian Ludwig Attersee est l'incarnation de l'idée d'œuvre d'art totale: il est à la fois peintre, écrivain, musicien, scénographe, artiste gestuel, designer et professeur d'art. Par ailleurs, Attersee représente l'Autriche, son pays natal, à la documenta de Kassel et à la Biennale de Venise. C'est un homme très affairé mais invariablement, le jeudi soir, il quitte Vienne pour Semmering. Il possède plusieurs résidences, mais sa somptueuse villa Alber, en parfait état de conservation et aménagée comme une demeure seigneuriale, est un exemple exceptionnel de ce que Attersee nomme lui-même son «univers attérien».

Vorhergehende Doppelseite, links: Das Pollerus-Haus vor der
Villa Alber stammt aus dem Jahr 1595 und ist das älteste erhaltene
Gebäude am Semmering.
Vorhergehende Doppelseite, rechts: Christian Ludwig Attersee bei
der Arbeit; die um 1890 erbaute Villa Alber.
Oben: Attersees Hunde Elvis und Priscilla.
Rechte Seite: der Künstler mit den Hunden in seinem Atelier.

Previous pages, left: The so-called Pollerus House, in front of Villa
Alber, dates from 1595 and is Semmering's oldest surviving building.
Previous pages, right: Christian Ludwig Attersee at work; the Villa
Alber, built about 1890.
Above: Attersee's dogs, Elvis and Priscilla.
Facing page: the artist in his studio at the Villa Alber, with his dogs.

Double page précédente, à gauche: Devant la villa Alber, la maison
Pollerus, bâtiment le plus ancien du Semmering, date de 1595.
Double page précédente, à droite: Christian Ludwig Attersee en
plein travail; la construction de la villa Alber remonte à l'année 1890.
Ci-dessus: Elvis et Priscilla, les deux chiens du maître de maison.
Page de droite: l'artiste, en compagnie de ses chiens, dans son atelier.

Oben: *Das offene Stiegenhaus – hier der erste Stock – ist denkmal-geschützt.*
Rechts: *das Vorzimmer im Erdgeschoß mit dem Gemälde eines belgischen Malers der Jahrhundertwende.*
Rechte Seite: *das Herrenzimmer mit einem französischen Art-déco-Lüster und englischen Art-déco-Möbeln.*

Above: *The broad open staircase – seen here from the first-floor landing – is under a conservation order.*
Right: *ground-floor hallway with a painting by a Belgian painter from the turn of the century.*
Facing page: *smoking room with a French Art Deco chandelier and English Art Deco furniture.*

Ci-dessus: *L'escalier, ici vu du premier palier, est classé; il dessert toute la maison.*
A droite: *l'antichambre, au rez-de-chaussée, avec le tableau d'un peintre belge du début du siècle.*
Page de droite: *le fumoir avec des meubles anglais et un lustre français, tous de style Art déco.*

Oben: *auf dem Tisch im Speisezimmer das von Attersee für Rosenthal entworfene Tee-Service »Teeforelle«.*
Rechts: *In der Bibliothek steht ein amerikanischer Billardtisch aus den fünfziger Jahren.*

Above: *Displayed on the dining room table is a tea service designed by Attersee for Rosenthal and entitled "Teeforelle" – "Tea Trout".*
Right: *A Fifties' American billiard table stands in the library.*

Ci-dessus: *sur la table de la salle à manger, le service à thé «Teeforelle» (truite-thé) dessiné par Attersee pour Rosenthal.*
A droite: *dans la bibliothèque, un billard américain datant des années cinquante.*

Alpen Interieurs   Christian Ludwig Attersee

Rechts: im Salon Wiener Möbel und das Gemälde »Erstes Grün« von Christian Ludwig Attersee von 1991/92.
Unten: Im Musikzimmer stehen ein Bösendorfer Flügel sowie Möbel aus den dreißiger und vierziger Jahren. An den Wänden hängen Plakate von Attersee-Ausstellungen.

Right: in the drawing room, Viennese furniture and the painting "Erstes Grün" (First Green) by Attersee dating from 1991/92.
Below: in the music room, a Bösendorfer grand piano, and furniture dating from the Thirties and Forties. Hanging on the wall are posters for Attersee exhibitions.

A droite: dans le salon, des meubles viennois et la peinture «Erstes Grün» (Premier Vert) de Christian Ludwig Attersee, datant de 1991/1992.
Ci-dessous: Dans la salle de musique, des meubles des années trente et quarante voisinent avec l'imposant piano à queue Bösendorfer. Des affiches des différentes expositions d'Attersee ornent les murs de la pièce.

His artist's smock is stained with layer upon layer of paint splashes, but he wears it like a royal robe. He has just turned 90 and is one of the greatest artists of our time: Balthus, master of Magic Realism. His full name has an aristocratic ring to it: Balthazar Count Klossowski de Rola. In 1977 his travels took him to the Gruyère Valley not far from Gstaad. And there, with the help of his art dealer and friend Pierre Matisse, he bought the "Grand Chalet". Built in 1754 and once a luxury hotel, the palatial wooden building boasts 30 rooms and 112 windows. Here he lives quietly with his second wife, the Japanese painter Setsuko Ideka. Their daughter Harumi trained under John Galliano, chief designer at Christian Dior, and is now designing her own jewellery collection. Harumi is her father's pride and joy, a fragile natural beauty, even more ravishing than the girls in his famous paintings.

Balthus

Seinen über und über mit Farbresten bedeckten Malerkittel trägt er wie ein Königsgewand. Er ist gerade 90 Jahre geworden und einer der großen Künstler unserer Zeit: Balthus, der Meister des magischen Realismus. Sein voller Name ist von vornehmen Klang: Balthazar Graf Klossowski de Rola. Ein bewegtes Leben führte ihn 1977 in das Gruyère-Tal unweit von Gstaad. Mit Hilfe seines Kunsthändlers und Freundes Pierre Matisse erwarb er das »Grand Chalet«, das aus dem Jahre 1754 stammt. Das aus Lärchenholz erbaute ehemalige Hotel ist ein gewaltiger Palast mit 30 Zimmern und 112 Fenstern. Hier lebt Balthus zurückgezogen mit seiner zweiten Frau, der Japanerin Setsuko Ideka, die Malerin ist wie er. Tochter Harumi hat bei John Galliano, dem Chefdesigner von Christian Dior, gelernt und entwirft nun ihre eigene Schmuck-Kollektion. Harumi ist Balthus' ganzer Stolz. Sie ist eine fragile, natürliche Schönheit, schöner noch als die Mädchen auf seinen berühmten Gemälden.

Dans sa blouse maculée de peinture, il a un port de roi, ce peintre de 90 ans, l'un des plus grands artistes de notre époque: Balthus, le maître du réalisme magique. Le pseudonyme de Balthus cache à vrai dire un nom aux consonances aristocratiques: Balthazar comte Klossowski de Rola. Après une existence agitée, le peintre se retira en 1977 dans la Gruyère. Par l'intermédiaire de son ami Pierre Matisse, le célèbre marchand d'art, il y fit l'acquisition d'un ancien hôtel bâti en 1754, le «Grand Chalet». Cette construction, où il vit désormais avec sa seconde femme, Setsuko Ideka, un peintre japonais, est un véritable palais en mélèze avec ses 30 pièces et ses 112 fenêtres. Sa fille Harumi s'est formée chez le modéliste vedette de Christian Dior, John Galliano, et crée maintenant ses propres collections de bijoux. Harumi est la grande fierté de Balthus: une beauté fragile, plus belle encore que toutes les jeunes filles qu'il a peintes.

Vorhergehende Doppelseite, links: *Das Grand Chalet ist das größte original erhaltene Chalet der Schweiz. In dem früheren Hotel logierte schon Victor Hugo. Am Gitter steht der Dalmatiner Fandor.*
Vorhergehende Doppelseite, rechts: *neben dem Foto von Balthus eine Bronzeskulptur von André Barrelier, ein Geschenk zum 88. Geburtstag; Balthus' Tochter Harumi (»Frühlingsblüte«); japanische Puppen.*
Linke Seite: *Die Kanarienvögel der Tochter »bewohnen« ein eigenes Zimmer.*
Oben: *im Eingangsbereich eine Sammlung von Regenschirmen. An der Wand hängen japanische Drucke der Hausherrin Setsuko, die einer Künstlerfamilie entstammt und ebenfalls Malerin ist.*

Previous pages, left: *The Grand Chalet is the largest chalet in Switzerland preserved in its original state. It was once a hotel with guests as celebrated as Victor Hugo. Standing at the gate is Fandor the dalmatian.*
Previous pages, right: *next to the photo of Balthus, a bronze sculpture by André Barrelier, an 88th birthday gift; Balthus' daughter, Harumi, whose name translates as "spring blossom"; Japanese dolls.*
Facing page: *Harumi's pet canaries have a room of their own.*
Above: *a collection of umbrellas in the entrance hall. Hanging on the wall are Japanese prints by Balthus' wife Setsuko, herself a painter from a family of artists.*

Double page précédente, à gauche: *Le Grand Chalet est le plus vaste chalet de Suisse conservé dans son état original. Cet ancien hôtel a hébergé des hôtes célèbres comme Victor Hugo. A la grille, Fandor, le dalmatien.*
Double page précédente, à droite: *à côté de la photo de Balthus, un bronze d'André Barrelier, offert pour ses 88 ans. Harumi («Fleur de printemps»), la fille de Balthus; des poupées japonaises.*
Page de gauche: *Les canaris de Harumi disposent d'une propre pièce.*
Ci-dessus: *dans l'entrée, une collection de parapluies; au mur, des estampes japonaises de la maîtresse de maison. Setsuko est issue d'une famille d'artistes et est également peintre.*

Oben: *der alte Fayenceofen aus dem 18. Jahrhundert in der Stube. Daneben hängt eine Arbeit von Setsuko. Die Künstlerin begeistert sich besonders für Stilleben und Interieurs.*
Rechte Seite: *das Speisezimmer. Für die fragile Blumendekoration aus dem eigenen Garten ist Setsuko zuständig.*

Above: *Next to the 18th-century faience tiled stove in the living room hangs a painting by Setsuko, whose special interests include still-lifes and interiors.*
Facing page: *the dining room, with Setsuko's delicate flower arrangement from the chalet's own garden.*

Ci-dessus: *la salle de séjour avec, à côté du poêle de faïence du 18e siècle, une œuvre de Setsuko. L'artiste est une passionnée de natures mortes et de décoration intérieure.*
Page de droite: *la salle à manger. La décoration florale provenant du propre jardin est exclusivement le domaine de Setsuko.*

Linke Seite: der rundum holzgetäfelte Salon mit Schweizer Möbel-
stücken. Über dem Sofa hängt »Colette im Profil« (1954) von
Balthus. Die schmiedeeisernen Lampen stammen aus Monte Calvello, wo der Maler einen Palazzo besitzt.
Oben: Detailansicht des Salons. Über dem Sekretär aus dem
18. Jahrhundert hängt »Der König der Katzen« (1935). Daneben
steht eine Büste von Alberto Giacometti.

Facing page: the entirely wood-panelled drawing room with Swiss
furniture. Above the sofa hangs "Colette in profile" (1954). The
wrought-iron lamps come from Monte Calvello, where the painter
owns a palazzo.
Above: detail of the drawing room. "The King of Cats" (1935) hangs
above the 18th-century secretaire; the bust is of Alberto Giacommetti.

Page de gauche: le salon avec ses boiseries en lambris et ses meubles
suisses. Au-dessus du canapé, un tableau de Balthus «Colette de profil» (1954). Les lampadaires en fer forgé viennent du Monte Calvello
où le peintre possède un château.
Ci-dessus: vue partielle du salon; au-dessus du secrétaire du
18e siècle, «Le Roi des chats» (1935) et, à côté, un buste d'Alberto
Giacometti.

Rechts: antike Marionetten aus Setsukos Heimat Japan.

Right: antique marionettes from Setsuko's native Japan.

A droite: de vieilles marionnettes du Japon, pays natal de Setsuko.

Unten: eines der zahlreichen, von Setsuko arrangierten Blumengestecke mit einem Harumi-Porträt von Balthus.

Below: one of Setsuko's many floral arrangements, with a drawing of Harumi by Balthus.

Ci-dessous: une des innombrables compositions florales de Setsuko, avec un portrait de Harumi dessiné par Balthus.

Links: Stilleben mit italienischer Stehlampe und einem Kinderporträt, das Harumi auf einem Flohmarkt fand.

Left: still-life with Italian standard lamp and portrait of a child, which Harumi discovered in a flea market.

A gauche: sur la table, une nature morte; à l'arrière-plan, un lampadaire italien et un portrait d'enfant déniché par Harumi sur un marché aux puces.

Rechts: Detailansicht der Küche, wo Monsieur Tchou, der chinesische Koch, herrscht.

Right: detail of the kitchen, the domain of Monsieur Chou, the Chinese cook.

A droite: un détail de la cuisine, domaine de Monsieur Tchou, le cuisinier chinois.

Rechte Seite: das kleine Sommerspeisezimmer mit einer Schweizer Anrichte und Queen-Anne-Stühlen.

Facing page: the little summer dining room with Swiss dresser and Queen Anne chairs.

Page de droite: la petite salle à manger d'été, avec son buffet suisse et ses chaises Queen Anne.

Alpen Interieurs   Balthus

Linke Seite und oben links: Im Atelier der Hausherrin steht vor dem bemalten rustikalen Bauernschrank ein Gemälde Setsukos, das die Chaiselongue in ihrem Schlafzimmer zeigt.
Oben rechts: das Schlafzimmer der Tochter mit Kinderspielzeug. Die Zeichnung auf dem Sessel ist ein Geschenk des Vaters.

Facing page and above left: In front of a painted rustic cupboard in Setsuko's studio is one of her paintings, showing the chaise longue in her bedroom.
Above right: Harumi's bedroom with toys. The drawing on the armchair is a gift from her father.

Page de gauche et ci-dessus à gauche: l'atelier de Setsuko. Devant l'armoire rustique peinte, est posé un de ses tableaux qui représente le canapé de repos de sa chambre.
Ci-dessus, à droite: la chambre de Harumi, avec des jouets d'enfant. Le dessin placé sur le fauteuil est un cadeau de son père.

As you drive from the village of Oberaudorf am Inn towards Tatzelwurm you will eventually come across Seebach, a hamlet consisting
of five long farmhouses. The oldest of these dates from the early 17th
century, the most recent was built in 1988. This, the home of the
Berger family, has a few rustic out-buildings that serve as holiday
homes for their summer visitors. Through the open front door, mighty
organ music flows out into the mountain landscape. Eleven-year-old
Hansi Berger is playing a fugue by Johann Sebastian Bach from
memory, under the watchful eye of his proud father. Hans Berger is
an organist and zither virtuoso who travels the world performing and
is often found researching ancient music in Munich's city library. It
was his love of music which caused him to hand over the farm to his
younger brother 28 years ago. Berger's favourite corner of the farm is
the former granary built in 1620. Here where the farm labourers used
to sleep, he invites his friends to convivial suppers, where food, drink,
laughter, card-playing and music-making are enjoyed in abundance.

Hans Berger

Wenn man von Oberaudorf am Inn hinauf nach Tatzelwurm fährt,
kommt man irgendwann nach Seebach, einem Gehöft von fünf
langgestreckten Bauernhäusern. Das älteste Gebäude stammt aus
dem frühen 17. Jahrhundert, das jüngste wurde 1988 erbaut. Hier
leben die Familie Berger und in ein paar urigen Ferienwohnungen
ihre Sommergäste. Die Haustür steht offen, gewaltige Orgelmusik
strömt hinaus in die Berglandschaft. Der elfjährige Hansi Berger
spielt eine Fuge von Johann Sebastian Bach. Er spielt sie ohne Noten, und der Vater schaut voller Stolz auf seinen Sohn. Hans Berger
ist Kirchenmusiker, spielt die Orgel, die Zither virtuos. Er reist mit
seiner Musik um die Welt und forscht in der Münchner Staatsbi-
bliothek nach alten Noten. Aus Liebe zur Musik hat er vor 28 Jahren zugunsten seines jüngeren Bruders auf den Hof verzichtet.
Bergers Lieblingsplatz ist der Getreidestadel aus dem Jahre 1620.
Wo früher die Knechte schliefen, lädt er sich gern Freunde ein.
Dann wird bei einer zünftigen Brotzeit gelacht und gezecht, Karten
gespielt und musiziert.

En montant du village de Oberaudorf am Inn vers celui de Tatzelwurm, on découvre la propriété de Seebach, cinq corps de ferme étirés
dont le plus ancien remonte au début du 17e siècle et le plus récent à
1988. C'est là que les Berger font partager leur vie de famille aux
hôtes venus passer leur vacances d'été dans quelques appartements
fidèlement restaurés. Par la porte ouverte, une musique puissante se
répand à flots dans la montagne. Hansi Berger, un garçon de onze
ans, est en train d'interpréter une fugue de Jean-Sébastien Bach à
l'orgue. Il joue sans partition et son père le regarde avec fierté. Hans
Berger est un grand organiste d'église ainsi qu'un virtuose de la cithare. Il donne des concerts dans le monde entier et effectue également des recherches sur la musique ancienne à la Bibliothèque natio-
nale de Munich. Il y a 28 ans, il a abandonné la propriété familiale à
son cadet pour pouvoir se consacrer à la musique. L'ancien grenier à
blé de 1620 est l'endroit préféré de Berger. Il aime y recevoir ses amis
pour de copieux repas campagnards.

Vorhergehende Doppelseite, rechts: Auf dem antiken Harmonium aus der nahegelegenen Kirche von Wall lernte Hans Berger als Junge spielen.
Linke Seite: Der Stadel wurde im Jahre 1620 aus Kiefern des eigenen Waldes gezimmert.
Oben: In dieser Kammer hatten Knechte, die bei der Ernte halfen, ihr Zuhause.
Folgende Doppelseite: Das Bett und einige der bäuerlichen Utensilien stammen aus dem 17. Jahrhundert.

Previous pages, right: As a child, Hans Berger learned to play the antique harmonium from the church in the nearby village of Wall.
Facing page: Pine from the woods on the farm's land was used to construct the barn in 1620.
Above: This room once provided sleeping quarters for the labourers who helped bring in the harvest.
Following pages: The bed and some of the farm implements date back to the 17th century.

Double page précédente, à droite: Hans Berger a appris, dès son enfance à jouer sur le vieil harmonium de l'église voisine de Wall.
Page de gauche: Le grenier a été construit en 1620 avec les pins de la propriété.
Ci-dessus: la mansarde où logeaient les journaliers pendant la saison des récoltes.
Double page suivante: Le lit et certains outils agricoles datent du 17e siècle.

Looming high above the Achental Valley in the Chiemgau, Bavaria, stands Marquartstein Castle, built by Marquart von Hohenstein in 1075. Since the late Eighties, the fortress has been the home of Konrad Otto Bernheimer, the internationally renowned art dealer who operates from London and Munich. Bernheimer was born in Venezuela, where his family emigrated during the Third Reich, but he spent his school years at the state school next to the castle. After this, he could not, in his own words, "let go of Marquartstein". Since the sale of the famous Bernheimer Palace in Munich, a symbol of the city and headquarters of the family business founded in 1864, the castle has become the family home. Although Bernheimer's professional life demands a great deal of travelling, this dynamic, cosmopolitan "bon viveur" likes to spend weekends at Marquartstein with his wife Barbara and their four daughters, whenever his schedule allows.

Konrad Otto Bernheimer

Hoch über dem Achental im Chiemgau thront die 1075 von Marquart von Hohenstein erbaute Burg Marquartstein. Seit Ende der achtziger Jahre ist sie im Besitz des international renommierten Kunsthändlers Konrad Otto Bernheimer (London/München). In Venezuela geboren, wohin seine Familie im Dritten Reich emigrierte, verbrachte Bernheimer seine Schulzeit in dem der Burg gegenüber gelegenen staatlichen Landschulheim. Seitdem hat ihn, so sagt er, »Marquartstein nicht mehr losgelassen«. Nach dem Verkauf des berühmten Bernheimer-Palais in München, einem Wahrzeichen der Stadt, das das Stammhaus des 1864 gegründeten traditionsreichen Familienunternehmens war, ist die Burg heute der Sitz der Familie. So oft es sein reiseintensives Kunsthändler-Leben erlaubt, verbringt der alerte, weltgewandte Genußmensch mit seiner Frau Barbara und den vier Töchtern die Wochenenden auf Marquartstein.

Très haut, au-dessus de la vallée d'Achental, dans le Chiemgau, trône le château de Marquartstein. Edifié en 1075 par Marquart von Hohenstein, il est depuis les années quatre-vingt propriété du marchand d'art mondialement connu Konrad Otto Bernheimer qui vit entre Londres et Munich. Né au Venezuela, où sa famille avait émigré sous le IIIe Reich, Bernheimer fit sa scolarité à l'école publique située près du château. Depuis, «Marquartstein ne m'a plus lâché», déclare-t-il. Après la vente du célèbre palais Bernheimer, un des emblèmes de Munich et maison mère de l'entreprise familiale fondée en 1864, ce château est devenu la résidence de la famille. Bernheimer est un homme alerte, un bon vivant plein de savoir-vivre qui, aussi souvent que ses affaires le lui permettent, passe les week-ends à Marquartstein avec sa femme Barbara et leurs quatre filles.

Vorhergehende Doppelseite, links: der große Festsaal.
Vorhergehende Doppelseite, rechts: Blick auf Burg Marquartstein.
Oben: Blick aus dem Herrenzimmer in die Zimmerflucht der Haupt-
wohnetage. Die Porträts zeigen die Ur-Ur-Großeltern Konrad Otto
Bernheimers.
Rechte Seite: Speisezimmer mit englischen Chinoiserie-Möbeln aus
der Zeit des Regency und Tellern aus dem sogenannten Pompadour-
Service.

Previous double page, left: view of the great banqueting hall.
Previous double page, right: views of Marquartstein Castle.
Above: view from the study into a series of rooms on the main resi-
dential floor. The portraits are of Konrad Otto Bernheimer's great-
great-grandparents.
Facing page: dining room with English Regency furniture in the Chinese style, and plates from the so-called Pompadour service.

Double page précédente, à gauche: la grande salle de réception.
Double page précédente, à droite: le château de Marquartstein.
Ci-dessus: depuis le bureau-fumoir, vue sur une enfilade de pièces au
bel étage. Les portraits représentent les trisaïeuls de Konrad Otto
Bernheimer.
Page de droite: la salle à manger, avec des meubles Régence anglaise
dans le goût chinois et des assiettes du service «Pompadour».

Links: eine Sammlung alter Schellackplatten mit allen bedeutenden Originalaufnahmen Enrico Carusos.

Left: collection of old shellac gramophone records with all the famous original recordings of Enrico Caruso.

A gauche: une collection de vieux disques en gomme-laque de tous les grands enregistrements originaux d'Enrico Caruso.

Rechts: das Fenster im Speisezimmer mit den Karaffen des Hausherrn.

Right: window in the dining room with some of Konrad Otto Bernheimer's carafes.

A droite: rebord de fenêtre de la salle à manger avec les carafes du maître de maison.

Linke Seite: ein Badezimmer mit Philippe-Starck-Badewanne. Der Paravent zeigt die Aufnahme einer Plakatwand in Israel von Tochter Teresa.

Facing page: a bathroom with Philippe Starck bathtub. On the screen, the photograph of a wall of posters in Israel, taken by daughter Teresa.

Page de gauche: une salle de bain avec une baignoire de Philippe Starck. Le paravent représente un mur d'affichage israélien photographié par Teresa, une des filles du maître des lieux.

Links: Kostüme aus dem Nachlaß von Rudolf Nurejew. Margot Fonteyn trug das Tutu in »Schwanensee«, als sie 1963 in London, Covent Garden, zum ersten Mal mit ihm tanzte.

Left: costumes from the estate of Rudolf Nureyev. The tutu was worn by Margot Fonteyn in "Swan Lake" when she partnered Nureyev for the first time at London's Covent Garden in 1963.

A gauche: des costumes de scène provenant de la succession du danseur Rudolf Noureev. Le tutu fut porté en 1963 par Margot Fonteyn dans le «Lac des cygnes» lorsqu'elle dansa pour la première fois avec lui au Covent Garden de Londres.

Links: im Badezimmer.

Left: in the bathroom.

A gauche: dans la salle de bain.

Rechts: Der Weinkeller ist der größte Schatz des Hausherrn, der ein ausgewiesener Weinkenner und -sammler ist.

Right: The master of the house is a well-known collector of fine wines whose cellar is his most treasured possession.

A droite: La cave à vins est le trésor le plus cher du maître des lieux, collectionneur expert.

The Caesetta da l'uors – "Bear Cabin" in Romansh – is a massive log cabin near St. Moritz, built in 1964 for the parents of the brilliant skier, film-maker and fashion entrepreneur Willy Bogner. In precisely the same year, Bogner Senior shot one of the world's largest bears, a four-metre-high Kodiak Island grizzly. Here, Bavarian cosiness and Swiss solidity mingle with Native American folk art. Bogner's mother, Maria, legendary company founder, and his Brazilian wife Sônia, a successful fashion designer, are jointly responsible for the interior design. Sadly, the family can only enjoy the fantastic view of Piz Corvatsch for a few weeks of the year. Occasionally, however, Willy Bogner shares the experience with a whole film team when, based at the "Bear Cabin", he shoots one of his famous ski films.

Sônia und Willy Bogner

Die Caesetta da l'uors – rätoromanisch für »Bärenhütte« – ist ein massives Blockhaus bei St. Moritz. Es wurde 1964 für die Eltern des genialen Skiartisten, Skifilmers und Mode-Unternehmers Willy Bogner erbaut, genau in dem Jahr, in dem der Senior einen der größten Bären der Welt erlegte, einen vier Meter großen Kodiak. Bayerische Gemütlichkeit und schweizerische Solidität mischen sich mit indianischer Volkskunst aus Amerika. Die Einrichtung besorgte Maria Bogner, die Mutter und legendäre Unternehmensgründerin, gemeinsam mit Sônia, Bogners brasilianischer Frau, einer erfolgreichen Modedesignerin. Leider genießt die Familie den phantastischen Blick auf den Piz Corvatsch nur wenige Wochen im Jahr. Gelegentlich aber teilt Willy Bogner ihn gleich mit einer ganzen Mannschaft, immer dann, wenn er von der »Bärenhütte« aus seine erfolgreichen Skifilme dreht.

La Caesetta da l'uors – «cabane de l'ours» en romanche – est un grand chalet bâti en 1964 par les parents de Willy Bogner, génial skieur, créateur de mode et réalisateur de films, près de Saint-Moritz. 1964 est l'année où le père de Willy tua un spécimen d'un des plus grands ours existants, un kodiak de quatre mètres. Le chalet marie avec bonheur confort bavarois, solidité suisse et art populaire américain. Deux femmes se sont occupées de l'aménagement intérieur: Maria Bogner, la légendaire créatrice d'entreprise et mère de Willy, et Sônia, sa femme, une modéliste brésilienne de renom. La famille ne dispose malheureusement que de quelques semaines par an pour profiter de la vue imprenable sur le Piz Corvatsch. De temps à autre, cependant, Willy Bogner partage le chalet avec toute une équipe de cinéma lorsqu'il vient tourner un de ses célèbres films de ski.

Vorhergehende Doppelseite, links: Sônia und Willy Bogner relaxen in ihrem Wohnzimmer an einem 300 Jahre alten Tisch; Detailansicht aus dem Eßzimmer; eine Wandlampe aus Weidengeflecht.
Vorhergehende Doppelseite, rechts: Die Kaminecke im 80 Quadratmeter großen Wohnraum ist besonders im Winter gemütlich. Die Cowboy-Parade auf dem Kaminsims ist eine Eisenplastik aus Arizona.
Unten: Das Fell des 1964 erlegten, vier Meter großen Bären hängt im Eßzimmer. Am Tisch finden zwölf Personen Platz.

Previous pages, left: Sônia and Willy Bogner relax beside a 300-year-old table; detail of the dining room; wickerwork wall light.
Previous pages, right: The chimney corner in the 80 square-metre living room is especially snug in winter. The cowboy parade on the mantlepiece is a wrought-iron sculpture from Arizona.
Below: The skin of a four-metre-high bear, killed in 1964, hangs in the dining room, where the dining table seats twelve people.

Double page précédente, à gauche: Sônia et Willy Bogner confortablement installés autour d'une table de 300 ans; vue partielle du séjour; une applique en osier.
Double page précédente, à droite: Le coin cheminée, dans le grand séjour de 80 mètres carrés, est agréable, surtout en hiver. La parade de cows-boys posée sur la tablette de la cheminée est une sculpture en fer originaire de l'Arizona.
Ci-dessous: La dépouille du grand kodiak tué en 1964 orne un des murs de la salle à manger. La table est assez grande pour recevoir douze personnes.

Vom Wohnzimmer aus blickt man auf den 3 451 Meter hohen Piz Corvatsch. Das Bild über dem Ledersofa stammt von dem indianischen Künstler Nieto aus Arizona, der Tisch ist aus Bayern und 300 Jahre alt.

The living room window looks out onto the 3 451-metre-high Piz Corvatsch. The painting above the leather sofa is by the Native American artist, Nieto of Arizona; the 300-year-old table comes from Bavaria.

Du séjour, on a vue sur le Piz Corvatsch, un sommet de 3 451 mètres d'altitude. Le tableau accroché au-dessus du canapé est de Nieto, un artiste indien originaire de l'Arizona. La table, qui a 300 ans, vient de Bavière.

The owners live and work in the financial world of London and Geneva, but their house at Commugny, close to Geneva, was originally a „grange", or large farmhouse, built in 1761. It still has the feel of a farmhouse, for, in carrying out the recent conversion, the architect Giuseppe Caruso has cleverly managed to emphasise the former use of the building. The unusual entrance hall with its 15-metre-high ceiling was once a passage leading from the living quarters to the cow shed, which dates from 1878. Giuseppe Caruso has retained the original beams and the openings through which hay and straw were pushed into the shed. Old-fashioned building materials underline the house's historical character: the treads of the asymmetrical wooden staircase date from the 18th century and were originally the floorboards of the sleeping quarters of a gold mine in the Piedmont. The living rooms have been kept simple, but carefully-chosen antiques and designer furniture add an air of refinement.

Ein Haus von Giuseppe Caruso

Die Besitzer arbeiten in der hochmodernen Finanzwelt von London und Genf, doch ihr 1761 errichtetes Haus in Commugny bei Genf war ursprünglich eine »grange«, ein großer Bauernhof. Das spürt man immer noch, denn der Architekt Giuseppe Caruso hat es verstanden, bei dem kürzlich erfolgten Umbau die frühere Nutzung des Hauses geschickt zu betonen. Der ungewöhnliche Eingangsbereich mit der 15 Meter hohen Decke war einst ein durchgehender Versorgungskorridor, der das Wohnhaus mit dem Kuhstall von 1878 verband. Giuseppe Caruso beließ die originalen Träger und auch die Öffnungen, durch die früher Heu und Stroh auf den Boden darüber geschoben wurden. Antike Materialien unterstreichen den historischen Charakter des Hauses: der Belag der Holztreppe stammt aus dem 18. Jahrhundert und lag ursprünglich in den Schlafräumen einer piemontesischen Goldmine. Die Wohnräume sind schlicht belassen, ausgesuchte Antiquitäten und Designmöbel setzen raffinierte Akzente.

Si les propriétaires vivent et travaillent dans le monde de la finance, à Londres et Genève, leur maison de Commugny près de Genève, édifiée en 1761, n'en était pas moins à l'origine une grange, et elle a su garder ce caractère. L'architecte a en effet souligné adroitement l'utilisation initiale du bâtiment lors des travaux de rénovation récents. La zone d'entrée inhabituelle avec son plafond haut de 15 mètres était autrefois un corridor d'approvisionnement qui reliait l'habitation à l'étable de 1878. Giuseppe Caruso a conservé les supports d'origine et aussi les ouvertures par lesquelles on amenait autrefois la paille et le foin sur le plancher situé au-dessus. Des matériaux anciens soulignent le caractère historique de la demeure: le plancher de l'escalier asymétrique date du 18e siècle et se trouvait à l'origine dans les dortoirs d'une mine d'or piémontaise. Les pièces d'habitation sont sobrement aménagées, mais des antiquités choisies avec discernement et des meubles design apportent des accents raffinés à l'ensemble.

Vorhergehende Doppelseite, links: *zwei Ansichten der »grange«.*
Vorhergehende Doppelseite, rechts: *eines der Schlafzimmer. Hier stehen direkt unter dem Dach ein bewegliches französisches Eisenbett aus dem 19. Jahrhundert und ein Kinderbett im Empire-Stil.*
Oben: *Das lichte Speisezimmer befindet sich in dem ehemaligen Innenhof der »grange« von 1761. Die rechte Wand zeigt noch den unverputzten Molasse-Stein der ursprünglichen Außenwand des Hauses.*
Links: *Blick von der steinernen Treppe im ehemaligen Korridor durch das Speisezimmer in den Wohnraum.*

Previous pages, left: *two views of the converted „grange".*
Previous pages, right: *one of the bedrooms. Standing directly under the roof are a 19th-century French iron bedstead on wheels, and an Empire-style child's cot.*
Above: *The light and airy dining room occupies the former inner courtyard of the 1761 „grange". The right-hand wall built of exposed Molasse stone was once an external wall and has been left unplastered.*
Left: *view of the stone staircase in what was once a corridor leading through the dining room into the living room.*

Double page précédente, à gauche: *deux vues de la grange.*
Double page précédente, à droite: *une des chambres à coucher. Située sous le toit, la pièce abrite un lit en fer forgé à roulettes français du 19e siècle et un lit d'enfant de style Empire.*
Ci-dessus: *Dans la salle à manger bien éclairée on peut encore contempler la molasse qui revêtait les murs extérieurs de la grange de 1761, en effet la pièce était autrefois une cour intérieure.*
A gauche: *vue de l'escalier de pierre sur la salle de séjour, le regard longe l'ancien corridor qui traverse la salle à manger.*

Oben: Der Wohnraum mit einem Louis-Treize-Kamin aus Beaune. Die Deckenbalken sind aus Kiefern- und Kastanienholz. Die Bodenplatten aus Beton und Rezina ahmen die Oberflächenstruktur antiker Steinböden nach. Sie wurden von einem Handwerker aus Beaune gefertigt. Eine »dormeuse« aus dem 19. Jahrhundert lädt zum Verweilen ein. Das afrikanische Waschbrett auf der Fensterbank steht im Gegensatz zur klassisch französischen Gestaltung des Raumes.
Rechts: Detailansicht in einem der Wohnzimmer.

Above: the living room with a Louis XIII fireplace from Beaune. The ceiling beams are pine and chestnut. The concrete and resin floor slabs, made by a craftsman from Beaune, imitate the surface structure of ancient stone floors. A 19th-century dormeuse, or chaise longue, is a comfortable place to linger. The African wash-board on the windowsill provides a counterpoint to the classic French style of the room.
Right: detail of one of the living rooms.

Ci-dessus: Le séjour et sa cheminée Louis XIII originaire de Beaune. Les poutres du plafond sont en pin et en châtaignier. Les dalles du sol, en béton et résine, imitent de par leur structure de surface les anciens revêtements de pierre. Elles ont été exécutées par un artisan de Beaune. Une «dormeuse» du 19e siècle invite à la détente. Sur l'appui de fenêtre une planche à laver africaine fait un clin d'œil au classique ameublement français.
A droite: un détail du séjour.

In the late Fifties, two Zurich doctors, father and son, were walking in the countryside of Switzerland's Saanenland region when they came across an old house built of spruce wood. The place was in ruins and being used as a hen-house. Having fallen in love with the view of Gstaad far below, the family bought the house and set to work. Today, the Chalet an der Matte ("chalet in the meadow"), originally built for a local farmer's family in about 1476, is the oldest restored building in the neighbourhood, as a wood analysis has revealed. The children, a brother and sister have now inherited it from their parents and collect local black and white ceramics and old engravings recounting the history of the Saanenland.

Chalet an der Matte

Ende der fünfziger Jahre entdeckten Vater und Sohn, beide Ärzte aus Zürich, auf einer Wanderung durch das Saanenland ein altes Haus aus Fichtenholz, eine Ruine, die als Hühnerstall genutzt wurde. Sie verliebten sich in den Blick auf das tief unter ihnen liegende Gstaad, kauften das Haus und begannen mit der Renovierung. Heute ist das ursprünglich für eine einheimische Bauernfamilie erbaute Chalet an der Matte (»Chalet an der Wiese«) das älteste restaurierte Anwesen der Umgebung. Eine Holzanalyse ergab eine Bauzeit um 1476. Bruder und Schwester haben es von den Eltern geerbt. Sie sammeln schwarzweiße Keramik aus der Gegend und alte Stiche, die die Geschichte des Saanenlandes dokumentieren.

A la fin des années cinquante, deux médecins de Zurich, un père et son fils, découvrent au cours d'une randonnée dans le Saanenland, un vieux chalet en bois d'épicéa tombant en ruine. Séduits par la vue sur Gstaad qui s'étend à leurs pieds, ils achètent la bâtisse convertie en poulailler et s'attellent aux travaux de restauration. Le Chalet an der Matte («le chalet sur le pâturage»), bâti à l'origine pour une famille paysanne du coin, est le plus ancien de la région à avoir été restauré. Une analyse du bois a permis de le dater de 1476. Les héritiers, un frère et une sœur, aiment collectionner des céramiques noires et blanches de la région et des gravures évocatrices de l'histoire du Saanenland.

Vorhergehende Doppelseite, links: *die Fassade des Chalets mit der typischen Balkenkonstruktion und dem Heidenkreuz am Giebel, anhand dessen das Haus um 1476 datiert werden kann; Kellertür mit Sommerlüftung; handgeschnitzter Briefkasten.*
Vorhergehende Doppelseite, rechts: *Seitenansicht mit dem 1958 angebauten, stilgetreuen Gästetrakt.*
Rechts: *Detail der Anrichte mit Geschirr aus Schramberg im Schwarzwald.*
Unten: *Den Wohnraum schmückt eine im 18. Jahrhundert bemalte Holzdecke. Truhe und Anrichte stammen aus dem Bündner Land.*

Previous pages, left: *front view of the chalet with typical timberwork and "pagan cross" on the gable, evidence that it was built around 1476; cellar entrance with ventilated door and wooden postbox.*
Previous pages, right: *side view with guest wing built in 1958, faithful to the original style.*
Right: *detail of the sideboard with a collection of Schramberg tableware from the Black Forest.*
Below: *The living room is enhanced by an 18th-century painted wooden ceiling; the chest and sideboard are from the Grisons.*

Double page précédente, à gauche: *la façade avec le poutrage et la croix païenne du pignon qui permet de dater la maison vers 1476; la porte de la cave avec son système d'aération estivale; la boîte à lettres sculptée main.*
Double page précédente, à droite: *une vue latérale du chalet, avec les chambres d'amis construites en 1958 dans le style d'origine.*
A droite: *un détail du buffet, avec une collection de faïences de Schramberg en Forêt Noire.*
Ci-dessous: *Le plafond du salon est décoré d'un lambris peint datant du 18e siècle; le coffre et le buffet sont de facture grisonne.*

Oben: Die Holzdecke im Elternschlafzimmer bildet ein leichtes Gewölbe. Die Truhe und die Stühle, sogenannte »Stabellen«, stammen
aus der Gegend.
Rechts: Blick vom Wohnraum in die Bibliothek. Rechts steht ein mit
Holz geheizter, grüner Kachelofen.

Above: The parents' bedroom has a gently vaulted wooden ceiling;
the chest and "Stabellen" (wooden chairs) were made locally.
Right: the library seen from the living room, with a tiled green wood-
burning stove on the right.

Ci-dessus: Le plafond lambrissé de la chambre des parents est légère-
ment voûté; le coffre et les «Stabellen» (tabourets) sont typiques de
la région.
A droite: la bibliothèque vue du salon; à droite, un poêle vert de
faïence chauffé au bois.

Oben: *ein rustikaler Klapptisch aus dem 18. Jahrhundert im Schlaf-zimmer. Der Hausherr nutzt ihn heute als Bücherregal und Schreib-tisch.*
Rechte Seite: *Detailansicht aus der Eingangshalle mit einem alten Mehlsack und einer Öllampe. Die Holzvertäfelung an der Wand ist altes Rauchholz aus dem offenen Kamin, der sich früher in der Ein-gangshalle befand und gleichzeitig als Räucherkammer für Schinken, Speck und Würste diente.*

Above: *In the bedroom is an 18th-century rustic folding table, now used by the owner as a desk and bookcase.*
Facing page: *detail of the entrance hall with an old flour bag and an oil lamp. The smoked-stained wood of the wall panels once sur-rounded the open fireplace which used to stand in the entrance hall and also served as a smokehouse for curing ham, bacon and sausages.*

Ci-dessus: *une table dépliante rustique du 18e siècle dans la chambre à coucher. Elle sert d'étagère pour les livres et de bureau au maître de maison.*
Page de droite: *le hall d'entrée avec un vieux sac de farine et une lampe à huile. Les murs sont lambrissés d'une boiserie qui tapissait l'ancienne cheminée située autrefois dans l'entrée, et où l'on fumait aussi le jambon, le lard et les saucisses.*

High on a hill above Montreux, the Zurich-born, New York-based industrial and interior designer Jean-Pierre Dovat has found sanctuary. Built in 1932, his chalet is called "Devadata", a Sanskrit word meaning "gift of God". That is also the way Dovat feels about his house, which he found in the mid-Eighties. At the time he had come to realise that, in order to savour his life of constant travel and creative hustle and bustle, he really needed a place to rest. Surrounded by objects of great beauty collected on his worldwide travels, Dovat takes refuge here as often as he can, though not often enough, and usually alone. He calls these "meditative days", when the magic of the place stirs him time and time again.

Jean-Pierre Dovat

Auf einem Hügel über Montreux hat der zur Zeit in New York lebende Züricher Industrie- und Interior-Designer Jean-Pierre Dovat sein Refugium gefunden. »Devadata« heißt das 1932 erbaute Chalet. Das ist Sanskrit und bedeutet »Geschenk Gottes«. Als solches empfindet Dovat sein Haus auch, das er Mitte der achtziger Jahre entdeckte. Damals hatte er erkannt, daß er einen Ruhepunkt braucht, um seine vielen Reisen und die kreative Unruhe seines Lebens wirklich genießen zu können. Umgeben von lauter schönen Stücken, die er von seinen Weltreisen mitbringt, zieht sich Dovat so oft es geht, aber doch zu selten, hierher zurück, meist allein. Das sind für ihn meditative Tage, sagt er, denn die Magie des Ortes berührt ihn immer wieder zutiefst.

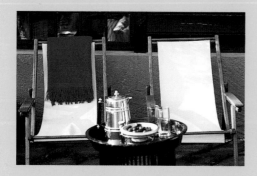

Jean-Pierre Dovat, décorateur et designer zurichois vivant à New York, a trouvé une magnifique retraite sur une hauteur qui domine Montreux. Son chalet, construit en 1932, a pour nom «Devadata», ce qui signifie «don de Dieu» en sanscrit. C'est d'ailleurs ainsi que Dovat ressent ce lieu qu'il a découvert dans les années quatre-vingt, à un moment où il éprouvait le besoin d'un havre de paix pour mieux apprécier, entre deux voyages, l'agitation créatrice de sa vie. Il s'y réfugie en solitaire le plus souvent possible – trop rarement pourtant à ses dires – au milieu de nombreux et beaux objets rapportés de ses périples autour du monde. C'est pour lui un lieu de méditation, plein de magie, qui ne cesse de l'impressionner.

Vorhergehende Seite: Bemooste Holzstufen führen zu dem 1932
erbauten Chalet in Caux am Genfer See.
Oben: Auf der wind- und wettergeschützten Veranda kann man das
ganze Jahr über Landschaft und Luft genießen. Der Tisch stammt aus
dem 18. Jahrhundert, der Regiestuhl ist von etwa 1938.
Rechts: Als Tischdecke für den Eßtisch dient eine Militärfahne. Der
Hochzeitsschrank stammt aus dem 18. Jahrhundert.
Rechte Seite: das Fenster zum Gästezimmer. Der Steinsockel des
Hauses ist in chinesischem Rot gestrichen. Dovat hat die Farbe selbst
gemischt und eigenhändig aufgetragen.

Previous page: Moss-covered wooden steps lead up to the chalet
built in 1932 at Caux on Lake Geneva.
Above: Sheltered from wind and weather, one can sit on the veranda
and enjoy the landscape and fresh air all the year round. The table is
18th-century, the folding chair dates from around 1938.
Right: A military flag serves as a cloth for the dining table. The
cabinet dates from the 18th century.
Facing page: the guest room window. The colour of the masonry is
based on Chinese red. Dovat mixed and applied the paint himself.

Page précédente: Des marches en bois moussues mènent au chalet
bâti en 1932 à Caux sur les bords du lac Léman.
Ci-dessus: De la véranda, bien abritée des intempéries, on peut
profiter du paysage et du bon air toute l'année. La table date du
18e siècle, la chaise vue à contre-jour, de 1938 environ.
A droite: La table de la salle à manger est nappée d'un drapeau mili-
taire, l'armoire nuptiale date du 18e siècle.
Page de droite: fenêtre ouvrant sur la chambre d'amis. Le soubassement du chalet est peint en rouge chinois, préparé et appliqué par
Dovat lui-même.

Oben und rechts: Die Gästezimmer sind mit mallorquinischen Stoffen ausgestattet. Die antiken Kissen stammen aus Ungarn, ein ländliches neogotisches Fauteuil kommt aus der Provence und ein Louis-XIII-Tisch aus Paris – so versammeln sich im Haus von Jean-Pierre Dovat Zeiten, Stile und Regionen.
Rechte Seite: Ein güldener Sonnenuntergang im Herbst: Am Horizont glänzt der Genfer See. Auf dem Fußboden liegt eine portugiesische Petit-point-Tapisserie. Ein amerikanischer Quilt aus dem späten 19. Jahrhundert ergänzt das kosmopolitische Ambiente.

Above and right: The guest rooms are furnished with Majorcan fabrics, the antique cushions are from Hungary, the rustic neo-gothic armchair from Provence, the Louis XIII table from Paris – Jean-Pierre Dovat's house is a pot-pourri of different periods, styles and regions.
Facing page: Lake Geneva sparkles on the horizon in the golden autumn sunset. On the floor is a Portuguese petit-point rug. A turn-of-the-century American quilt completes the cosmopolitan ambience.

Ci-dessus et à droite: Les chambres d'amis sont garnies de tissus majorquins; les vieux coussins proviennent de Hongrie, un fauteuil de style néogothique rustique vient de Provence, une table Louis XIII, de Paris. La maison de Jean-Pierre Dovat est une harmonie d'époques, de styles et de régions.
Page de droite: lumière mordorée dans le crépuscule automnal; à l'horizon, scintille le lac Léman. Un tapis au petit point portugais recouvre le sol. Une courtepointe américaine de la fin du 19e siècle parachève l'atmosphère cosmopolite des lieux.

For a century, the rectangular, wooden gamekeeper's cottage has stood in an idyllic woodland clearing near St. Gallen, 700 metres above sea level. The Gnädingers, Magi and Martin Senior, who run a workshop making architectural models, bought the place in 1989 when the last survivor of the gamekeeper's family moved into a retirement home. Today, the three sons of the family occupy the house. Martin, Pascal and Florian, all in their early twenties, are mad about architecture and fill the place with their music. Their parents live a few hundred metres away, in an old shoemaker's house.

Familie Gnädinger

Schon seit einem Jahrhundert steht das ehemalige Wildhüterhaus auf der Wiese einer verwunschenen Waldlichtung in der Nähe von St. Gallen, 700 Meter über dem Meeresspiegel. Die Gnädingers, Magi und Martin senior, betreiben ein Architekturmodellbau-Atelier und erwarben den Holzständerbau mit quadratischem Grundriß im Jahre 1989, als das letzte Familienmitglied der Wildhüterfamilie in ein Altersheim zog. Heute leben hier die Söhne Martin, Pascal und Florian, allesamt Anfang zwanzig, architektur- und musikversessen. Die Eltern wohnen wenige hundert Meter entfernt in einem alten Schuhmacherhaus.

Bâtie à 700 mètres d'altitude dans une magnifique clairière des environs de Saint-Gall, cette maison de garde-chasse centenaire est de plan carré, avec une solide charpente en bois. Les propriétaires, Magi et Martin Gnädinger, qui dirigent un bureau de maquettisme architectural, en ont fait l'acquisition en 1989, lorsque le dernier membre de la famille du garde-chasse est parti vivre dans une maison de retraite. La demeure, toujours pleine de musique, est occupée aujourd'hui par leurs fils, Martin, Pascal et Florian, tous trois âgés d'une vingtaine d'années et passionnés d'architecture. Les parents habitent une ancienne maison de bottier, à moins de cent mètres de là.

Linke Seite: *Familie Gnädinger; die Garage aus Sichtbeton bildet einen reizvollen Kontrast zum Wohnhaus.*
Oben: *Vor der dunkelblau gestrichenen Außenwand aus Holzbohlen befindet sich eine Plexiglas-Haut. Sie verleiht dem um die Jahrhundertwende errichteten und 1991 von dem Schweizer Architekten Beat Consoni umgebauten Haus eine futuristische Note.*
Rechts: *Das ehemalige Wildhüterhaus steht auf einer romantischen Waldlichtung.*

Facing page: *the family Gnädinger; the exposed concrete garage provides an interesting contrast with the house.*
Above: *The transparent plexiglas skin placed in front of the external wall of dark blue painted wooden planks lends a futuristic touch to the house, built at the turn of the century and remodelled in 1991 by the Swiss architect Beat Consoni.*
Right: *The former gamekeeper's cottage stands in a romantic woodland clearing.*

Page de gauche: *la famille Gnädinger; le garage en béton brut de décoffrage contraste avec la maison.*
Ci-dessus: *L'architecte suisse Beat Consoni, chargé de transformer la maison en 1991, lui a donné une allure futuriste en tendant une pellicule de plexiglas sur le mur extérieur peint en bleu foncé.*
A droite: *L'ancienne maison de garde-chasse est nichée dans une clairière romantique.*

Rechts: So kompakt das Haus von außen wirkt, so weiträumig ist es innen. Die ursprüngliche Zimmeranordnung wurde auf allen drei Ebenen durch eine offene Raumfolge ersetzt.
Unten: der Durchblick vom Eßzimmer in die Küche mit ihrem langen Fensterband. Die Kunst im Haus stammt von Monika Gnädinger, der kreativen Hausherrin.

Right: The interior spaciousness of the house belies its compact external appearance. The original room layout has been replaced by an open-plan arrangement over all three floors.
Below: Looking through the dining area we see the kitchen with its long ribbon window. The paintings are by Monika Gnädinger, creative mistress of the house.

A droite: Autant la maison paraît ramassée de l'extérieur, autant elle est spacieuse à l'intérieur. L'ancienne distribution des pièces a fait place à une suite d'espaces ouverts sur trois niveaux.
Ci-dessous: On aperçoit depuis la salle à manger la cuisine avec son long bandeau de fenêtre. Toutes les peintures sont l'œuvre de Monika Gnädinger, la maîtresse de maison.

Einfach und funktional ist die gesamte Einrichtung des Hauses.
Markant wirkt der in eine rohe Betonwand eingefügte moderne
rotlackierte Holzofen. Die Betonwand dient als Wärmespeicher und
-verteiler.

All the furnishings are simple and functional. A striking feature is the
modern red-enamelled wood-burning stove set in a wall of rough concrete. The concrete wall serves to accumulate and radiate heat.

L'aménagement intérieur est simple et fonctionnel. A remarquer en
particulier: le poêle verni rouge, encastré dans un mur en béton brut,
qui permet de récupérer et de diffuser la chaleur.

In 1567 Archduke Karl of Styria began building Schloß Ebenthal. However, it was only after two extensive reconstructions – in 1675 and between 1705 and 1730 – that the baroque palace assumed its present form. Ebenthal has belonged to the Goëss family since 1704 and was inherited by Leopold, Count Goëss in 1953. Together with his Countess, Dora, the Count, a former head of the Carinthian government and a member of the European Parliament, manages the vast family estate. The 38 hectare park surrounding the Schloß is laid out in English style; the lawns are interspersed with shrubs and clumps of trees, and there is a large area of forest. The view of gently tamed nature seen from the magnificent ballroom would make the perfect setting for a film.

Leopold Graf Goëss

Im Jahre 1567 begann Erzherzog Karl von Steiermark mit dem Bau von Schloß Ebenthal. Aber erst nach zwei umfangreichen Umbaumaßnahmen – 1675 und von 1705 bis 1730 – entstand das Barockschloß in seiner bis heute erhaltenen Anlage. Seit 1704 befindet sich Ebenthal im Besitz der Grafen Goëss. Durch Erbrecht gelangte es 1953 in den Besitz von Dr. Leopold Graf Goëss. Der ehemalige Landeshauptmann von Kärnten und Mitglied des Europaparlaments kümmert sich zusammen mit seiner Frau, Dora Gräfin Goëss, um die Verwaltung des ausgedehnten Familienbesitzes. Das Schloß umgibt ein etwa 38 Hektar großer englischer Park. Weite Rasenflächen wechseln mit Büschen und Baumgruppen, ein großer Teil ist Forstwald. Der Blick vom prachtvollen Festsaal in die lässig gebändigte Natur ist filmreif.

L'archiduc Karl von Steiermark entreprit l'édification du château d'Ebenthal en 1567. Mais celui-ci ne prit sa forme définitive qu'à la suite de grandes transformations réalisées en 1675, puis entre 1705 et 1730. Ce château de style baroque est depuis 1704 propriété des comtes Goëss, et l'actuel comte, Leopold, en a hérité en 1953. Ancien grand administrateur de la Carinthie et député au parlement européen, il gère aujourd'hui les nombreux biens de la famille, assisté dans cette tâche par sa femme Dora. Le parc de 38 hectares est dessiné à l'anglaise : des pelouses alternent avec des buissons et des boqueteaux, la majeure partie a été aménagée en forêt. La grande salle de réception offre une magnifique perspective, digne d'un décor de film, sur la nature environnante.

Vorhergehende Doppelseite, links: *Der heitere Freskensaal mit himmlischen Motiven und einem Ochsenauge.*

Vorhergehende Doppelseite, rechts: *Die Schloßbesitzer Dr. Leopold Graf Goëss und Dora Gräfin Goëss; die Westfassade des Schlosses vom Park aus gesehen.*

Oben: *Um 1748 schuf der in Kärnten und im Friaul berühmte Klagenfurter Maler Josef Ferdinand Fromiller (1693–1760) die Dekorationen des Freskensaals. Im Zentrum der Götterversammlung thront Zeus auf einem schwebenden Adler.*

Rechte Seite: *Das Familienzimmer schmücken lebensgroße Porträts von drei Generationen der Familie Goëss. Der Wiener Hofmaler Johann Peter Kobler schuf sie ab 1739.*

Folgende Doppelseite: *Die Schloßbibliothek umfaßt etwa 3 500 historische Bände.*

Previous pages, left: *the splendid Hall of Frescoes with heavenly motifs and an "œil de boeuf" window.*

Previous pages, right: *owners of Schloß Ebenthal, Count Leopold and Countess Dora Goëss; the west façade of the Schloß seen from the park.*

Above: *The Hall of Frescoes was created in about 1748 by Josef Ferdinand Fromiller (1693–1760), a painter born in Klagenfurt and famed throughout Carinthia and Friuli. Enthroned on a flying eagle, Zeus presides over a gathering of the Gods.*

Facing page: *part of the family room, the walls lined with life-size portraits of three generations of family members, painted by Johann Peter Kobler. Kobler was a painter at the Viennese court.*

Following pages: *The library contains some 3 500 history books.*

Double page précédente, à gauche: *la belle salle des fresques avec ses motifs mythologiques et son œil-de-bœuf.*

Double page précédente, à droite: *les maîtres des lieux, le comte Leopold Goëss et sa femme Dora; la façade occidentale du château, vue du parc.*

Ci-dessus: *Les fresques ont été exécutées vers 1748 par le peintre Josef Ferdinand Fromiller (1693–1760), fort connu non seulement à Klagenfurt mais dans tout le Frioul et en Carinthie. Au centre, Zeus dressé sur un aigle.*

Page de droite: *un coin de la salle de réunion familiale avec ses peintures grandeur nature représentant trois générations de la dynastie Goëss, exécutées à partir de 1739 par le peintre de la cour de Vienne Johann Peter Kobler.*

Double page suivante: *La bibliothèque compte environ 3 500 ouvrages historiques.*

He is a world-renowned conductor and highly successful entrepreneur, both famous and infamous for his aggressive political and ecological commitment. Recently married to his second wife, an elegant Roman, and the father of two grown-up sons, Enoch Baron Guttenberg divides his time between his ancestral home in Franconia and his residence in Chiemgau where the amateur choir of 100 voices he has presided over since he was 21 owes its worldwide renown to Guttenberg. He also owns the "Maierhaus", which was built in 1887, and converted by Guttenberg, according to his own requirements. The front section which now contains offices, has the appearance of a fine country house. The Choir members celebrate with the Baron, affectionately known as "Our Guttai". Their occasional festivals of choral music are held on the former threshing floor.

Enoch Freiherr zu Guttenberg

Als Dirigent genießt er Weltruf, als Unternehmer arbeitet er äußerst erfolgreich und für sein kämpferisches politisches und ökologisches Engagement ist er berühmt und berüchtigt. Enoch Freiherr zu Guttenberg, in zweiter Ehe frisch mit einer eleganten Römerin verheiratet, ist Vater von zwei erwachsenen Söhnen. Er lebt – neben dem Stammsitz der Familie in Franken – einige Tage in der Woche im Chiemgau. Dort leitet er die Chorgemeinschaft, einen hundertköpfigen Laienchor, dem Guttenberg seit seinem 21. Lebensjahr vorsteht und der ihm seinen Weltruhm verdankt. Im Jahre 1981 kaufte er das 1887 errichtete »Maierhaus« und baute es nach seinen Bedürfnissen um. Der vordere Gebäudeteil, in dem sich die Büros befinden, gleicht einem Großbürgerhaus. In der umgebauten Tenne feiert der Baron gelegentlich mit dem Chor, dessen Mitglieder ihn beinahe zärtlich »unseren Guttai« nennen.

Le baron Enoch zu Guttenberg est un chef d'orchestre et un chef de chœur de renommée mondiale, un brillant entrepreneur et un homme célèbre et critiqué pour ses prises de position politiques et écologiques. Remarié depuis peu avec une élégante Italienne, originaire de Rome, père de deux enfants adultes, il vit dans la résidence familiale de Franconie. Mais il passe quelques jours par semaine dans une petite ville dans le Chiemgau, siège de la chorale (un ensemble de 100 choristes amateurs) dont il est le chef depuis l'âge de 21 ans, et qui lui doit sa notoriété. Mais il a une autre raison d'y venir: sa maison, «Maierhaus», construite en 1887, est pour lui un véritable refuge où il aime vivre et travailler. Guttenberg a fait transformer en 1981 l'ancienne ferme du château pour ses besoins. La partie avant du bâtiment, qui abrite à présent les bureaux, ressemble à une maison bourgeoise. La chorale se réunit à l'occasion dans l'ancienne aire de battage, à l'invitation de celui qu'elle nomme affectueusement «notre Guttai».

Vorhergehende Doppelseite, links: der Dirigent Enoch Freiherr zu
Guttenberg; das schmiedeeiserne Tor zum Garten.
Vorhergehende Doppelseite, rechts: In der ehemaligen Tenne ist
heute ein Fest- und Theatersaal untergebracht.
Oben: der große Salon im ehemaligen Stall.
Rechts: Ein Orgelschrank aus dem Barock dient als Bar.
Rechte Seite: Die Tapisserien im Speisezimmer stammen aus dem
18. Jahrhundert und wurden von einem Kirchenmaler aus dem
Chiemgau durch Wandmalereien ergänzt.

Previous pages, left: the conductor, Enoch Baron Guttenberg; the
wrought-iron garden gate.
Previous pages, right: The former threshing floor is now a festival
hall and theatre.
Above: large drawing room in the former stable.
Right: This baroque organ case is now used as a bar.
Facing page: The 18th-century tapestries in the dining room are offset
by the murals of a church painter from Chiemgau.

Double page précédente, à gauche: le baron Enoch zu Guttenberg;
le portail en fer forgé du jardin.
Double page précédente, à droite: L'ancienne aire de battage abrite
maintenant une salle des fêtes et un théâtre.
Ci-dessus: le grand salon dans l'étable désaffectée.
A droite: Une console d'orgue de style baroque fait office de bar.
Page de droite: Dans la salle à manger, les peintures murales, dues
à un peintre d'église du Chiemgau, complètent les tapisseries du
18e siècle.

Linke Seite: *Georg Enoch zu Guttenberg sammelt Figuren, Objekte, Zeichnungen, Literatur und anderes über seinen Namenspatron, den Heiligen Georg.*
Oben: *In den Vitrinen des großen Salons befinden sich Rokoko-Figuren und wertvolle Erstausgaben. Der Sekretär stammt aus dem Barock, der Konsoltisch aus dem Rokoko.*
Rechts: *ein Porzellan-Ensemble nach dem Gemälde »Flötenkonzert Friedrichs II. in Sanssouci« von Adolph von Menzel (1815–1905).*

Facing page: *Georg Enoch zu Guttenberg collects figures, objects, drawings, literature and other artefacts relating to Saint George, his pat-ron saint.*
Above: *The display cabinets in the main drawing room contain rococo figurines and first editions. The secretaire is baroque and the console table rococo.*
Right: *a reproduction in porcelain of the painting by Adolph von Menzel (1815–1905), "Frederick II's flute concerto at Sanssouci".*

Page de gauche: *Georg Enoch zu Guttenberg collectionne des figurines, des objets, des dessins et des livres sur saint Georges, son patron.*
Ci-dessus: *Les vitrines du grand salon présentent des figurines rococo et des éditions princeps. Le secrétaire est baroque, la console, rococo.*
A droite: *une collection de porcelaines dont les motifs sont inspirés d'un tableau d'Adolph von Menzel (1815–1905), «Concert de flûtes de Frédéric II à Sans-Souci».*

In the Grisons Alps, not far from Klosters, stands Haus Casanna, a 300-year-old alpine log building with elaborate wood carving. Typical of the Wals Valley, it takes its name from the view of the Casanna mountain. Here, since 1979, Zurich's star hair stylist Rudolf "Ruedi" Haene has indulged in his favourite hobbies, collecting antiques and modern alpine kitsch, and decorating and restoring the holiday home where he and his friends spend as much time as possible. He sometimes rents the house out to visitors. In all its alpine glamour, Haene's home reflects his own personal style: frivolous and irreverent. White is the predominant colour in all the rooms. In Haene's opinion, this shows the dark wood to its best advantage, offsetting the green of the forest in summer and mirroring the snow-covered landscape in winter.

Rudolf Haene

In der Nähe von Klosters liegt das 300 Jahre alte Walser Strickhaus in den Bündner Alpen. Wegen des Blicks auf den gleichnamigen Berg wird es »Haus Casanna« genannt. Seit 1979 frönt hier der Züricher Starfriseur Rudolf »Ruedi« Haene seinen liebsten Hobbys, dem Sammeln von altem und neuem Alpenkitsch sowie dem Dekorieren und Restaurieren seines Hauses. Er nutzt es, so oft es geht, mit Freunden als Feriendomizil, vermietet es aber auch zeitweise. Den Stil des Hauses bezeichnet er als »Alpenglamour«, frivol und respektlos – wie er sich selbst auch gern sieht. In allen Räumen dominiert die Farbe Weiß. So kommen die dunklen Holztöne, im Sommer das Grün der Wälder und im Winter die Schneelandschaft gut zur Geltung.

Non loin de Klosters, petite ville des Grisons, se trouve un chalet tricentaire, une ancienne «Walser Strickhaus» ou «tricoterie valaisane», baptisé «Haus Casanna», du nom de la montagne voisine. Un coiffeur vedette zurichois, Rudolf «Ruedi» Haene, s'y adonne depuis 1979 à ses passions: la collection de toutes sortes d'objets kitsch des Alpes ainsi que la restauration et la décoration de sa maison, où il passe le plus souvent possible ses vacances, entouré d'amis. Il lui arrive même de la louer, quelques semaines par an. Il qualifie son style de «glamour alpin», frivole et irrespectueux, tout à fait à son image, comme il le prétend lui-même. La couleur dominante des pièces est le blanc, qu'il a choisi pour mettre en valeur les tons foncés du bois, le vert de la forêt en été et le paysage enneigé en hiver.

Vorhergehende Seite: Die Haustür wurde nach alten Vorbildern von einem einheimischen Schreiner neu gearbeitet. Edelweiß-Motive, Blechwappen und alte Skier sind Mitbringsel von Freunden.
Oben und rechts: Auf der windgeschützten überdachten Terrasse mit Sicht auf das Alpenpanorama sorgen Feuerholz, ein Vogelhäuschen, Buchsbäume, weiße Kissen, Jagdtrophäen und – wenn's kalt wird – ein Heizstrahler für Gemütlichkeit.
Rechte Seite: Auch den verspielten Pavillon in einer Gartenecke hat der Hausherr selbst entworfen. Die Jagdtrophäen hat er, da er selbst kein Jäger ist, als Dutzendware in Antikläden erstanden.

Previous page: The front door was remodelled in antique style by a local joiner. The edelweiss, metal shields and old skis are souvenirs from friends.
Above and right: Enclosed and sheltered from the wind, the terrace offers a panorama of the Alps. Firewood, an aviary, box shrubs, white cushions, hunting trophies and – in cold weather – an electric wall heater all add cosiness.
Facing page: The delightful gazebo in a corner of the garden was designed by the owner himself. Haene's hunting trophies were hunted down in job lots in antique shops – which is as near to the hunt as he is likely to be getting.

Page précédente: La porte d'entrée a été restaurée d'après des modèles d'un ancien menuisier de la région. Les edelweiss, le blason en fer-blanc et les vieux skis sont des cadeaux offerts par des amis.
Ci-dessus et à droite: La terrasse couverte, bien abritée, permet d'admirer le panorama des Alpes. Des bûches, un nichoir, des buis en pot, des coussins blancs, des trophées de chasse et un radiateur électrique pour les journées froides assurent son confort.
Page de droite: Le pavillon ludique du jardin est une autre création du maître des lieux. Celui-ci, qui n'est pas chasseur, a déniché les trophées dans des magasins de brocante.

Oben: *Prunkstück im gemütlichen Salon ist der Spiegel aus der Zeit Ludwigs XVI. Die Stühle hat der Hausherr selbst abgelaugt, das Hirschgeweih persönlich geweißt.*
Rechts: *An den Wänden des Salons befinden sich Fundstücke aus Züricher und neapolitanischen Antikläden.*

Above: *A Louis XVI mirror takes pride of place in the cosy drawing room. Haene himself stripped the chairs and whitewashed the antlers.*
Right: *The drawing room walls are adorned with bric-à-brac picked up in antique shops in Zurich and Naples.*

Ci-dessus: *Le plus bel objet du salon est le miroir Louis XVI. Le maître de maison a lui-même lessivé les tabourets et blanchi la ramure de cerf.*
A droite: *aux murs du salon, des objets dénichés à Zurich et chez des antiquaires de Naples.*

Alpen Interieurs   Rudolf Haene

Rechts: Das Himmelbett im sogenannten »weißen Gästezimmer« wurde nach einem Entwurf des Hausherrn angefertigt. Die Bettwäsche stammt teilweise aus dem Fundus des Hauses, aber auch von Ikea.
Unten: An die Küche schließt sich das Eßzimmer an. Über dem Orchideenstock hängt ein üppiger Kristall-Leuchter aus der Zeit Napoleons III. Im antiken Spiegel kann man bei gutem Wetter die Alpen sehen.

Right: The owner of the house designed the four-poster bed in the so-called "white" guest bedroom. Some of the bed linen comes from the original house linen supply, some from Ikea.
Below: Adjoining the kitchen is the dining room. Above a pot of orchids is a crystal chandelier from the time of Napoleon III. On a clear day, a view of the Alps is reflected in the antique mirror.

A droite: Le lit à baldaquin de la «chambre blanche» est une création du propriétaire. Une partie de la literie se trouvait dans la maison, le reste vient d'Ikea.
Ci-dessous: Dans la salle à manger attenante à la cuisine, un lustre en cristal de l'époque Napoléon III est suspendu au-dessus d'une orchidée. Par beau temps, on peut voir le paysage alpin se réfléchir dans le miroir ancien.

For ten years, the well-travelled designer Barbara Hammerstein had looked longingly at her dream house, the Berghof, set 1 000 metres high in a remote position with a view of the Zugspitze, close to her home town of Garmisch in Bavaria. In 1983 she received the decisive phone call and immediately bought the property. Built in 1665, the farmhouse originally stood in an alpine pasture, providing shelter for dairy cows. In those days the tenant farmers had to pay rent to the diocese of Freising. Barbara Hammerstein has 600 square metres of living space with a total of 15 rooms, some of which she rents out to friends and holidaymakers. In the garden are two "Stadel", old wooden barns: One is the owner's ceramics workshop, the other, a little shop selling interior design accessories from around the world. In her own self-assured way, Barbara Hammerstein has conquered the world, but her real home is here in Upper Bavaria.

Barbara Hammerstein

Zehn Jahre lang hat die in Garmisch geborene Kosmopolitin Barbara Hammerstein mit dem »Berghof« geliebäugelt. Ihr Traumhaus mit Blick auf die Zugspitze liegt einsam, 1 000 Meter hoch. 1983 bekam sie den entscheidenden Anruf und kaufte das Anwesen sofort. Der 1665 erbaute Bergbauernhof war ursprünglich eine Senne, also ein Hof, auf dem Milchkühe gehalten wurden. Die Lehnbauern mußten ihren Tribut an das Bischofstum Freising abführen. Barbara Hammerstein verfügt über eine Wohnfläche von 600 Quadratmeter und insgesamt 15 Zimmer, von denen sie einige an Freunde und Feriengäste vermietet. Im Bauerngarten stehen zwei alte Holzstadel. Der eine dient der Hausherrin als Keramikwerkstatt, in dem anderen Stadel betreibt sie einen kleinen Laden für Einrichtungsgegenstände und Accessoires aus aller Welt. Selbstbewußt hat Barbara Hammerstein auf ihre Art die Welt erobert, aber hier in Oberbayern, da ist sie zu Hause.

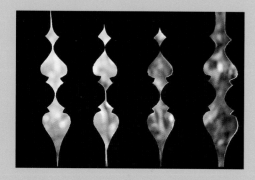

Pendant dix ans, Barbara Hammerstein – une architecte d'intérieur cosmopolite de Garmisch, en Bavière – convoite la maison de ses rêves, un chalet isolé, situé à 1 000 mètres d'altitude, face au Zugspitze. En 1983 on la prévient par téléphone que le chalet est mis en vente. Elle l'achète immédiatement. Cette bâtisse qui date de 1665 était à l'origine une «Senne», une laiterie d'alpage. Dans l'ancien temps, les paysans du coin devaient payer tribut à l'archevêché de Freising. Le chalet comprend 600 mètres carrés de surface habitable et 15 pièces en tout, dont quelques-unes sont louées par Barbara Hammerstein à des amis ou à des vacanciers. Dans le jardin, se trouvent deux «Stadels», dont l'un a été transformé en atelier de poterie et l'autre, en boutique. Barbara Hammerstein y vend des décorations d'intérieur et des accessoires de toutes les régions du monde. Si Barbara Hammerstein a conquis le monde à sa manière, c'est ici, en Haute-Bavière, qu'elle se sent vraiment chez elle.

Eingangsseite, links: *Barbara Hammerstein mit Windlichtern aus verrosteten Kartoffelreiben; ein dekorativ geschnitztes Geländer.*
Eingangsseite, rechts: *traditionelles altes Balkongeländer.*
Vorhergehende Doppelseite: *Blick vom Balkon in der ersten Etage des Berghofs auf die 2 000 Meter hohe Dreitorspitze. Vorne im Bild ein alter Nähkorb.*
Oben: *Sommerwiese vor dem Haus mit von Barbara Hammerstein selbstgebauten Hirschen aus Holzbalken. Die Hausherrin ist Innenarchitektin und verbrachte jahrelang mehrere Monate im Jahr in Saudi-Arabien. Heute arbeitet sie von Garmisch aus.*

First pages, left: *Barbara Hammerstein with lanterns made from rusty potato graters; a decoratively carved balcony rail.*
First pages, right: *traditional old balcony rails.*
Previous pages: *view of the 2 000–metre-high Dreitorspitze from the first-floor balcony of the Berghof; in the foreground, an old sewing basket.*
Above: *the meadow in front of Barbara Hammerstein's house, with deer fashioned by the owner herself from wooden beams. An interior designer, she used to spend several months a year in Saudi Arabia, but is currently working from Garmisch.*

Première double page, à gauche: *Barbara Hammerstein et devant elle, des photophores fabriqués avec des râpes à pommes de terre rouillées; une balustrade décorative en bois sculpté.*
Première double page, à droite: *une vieille balustrade de style traditionnel.*
Double page précédente: *vue sur le Dreitorspitze (2 000 mètres d'altitude), depuis le balcon du premier étage. Au premier plan, une ancienne corbeille à ouvrage.*
Ci-dessus: *Dans la prairie d'été, Barbara Hammerstein a elle-même réalisé ces cerfs à partir de poutres en bois. La maîtresse des lieux est architecte d'intérieur. Longtemps, elle a passé plusieurs mois par an en Arabie Saoudite. Aujourd'hui, elle exerce sa profession depuis Garmisch.*

Rechts: Große Steine beschweren die hölzernen Dachschindeln.
Unten: Ansicht des Berghofs vom Wald aus.

Right: The wooden shingles of the roof are weighted down by large stones.
Below: view of the Berghof from the forest.

A droite: De grosses pierres maintiennent les bardeaux du toit.
Ci-dessous: la maison vue depuis la forêt.

Rechts: das Kaminzimmer mit der hohen Gewölbedecke, die von der offenen Feuerstelle der alten Küche rußverschwärzt ist. Über dem Kamin hängen alte Mistelkronen. Jedes Jahr kommt zum Jahreswechsel eine neue dazu.
Unten: In der Stube steht links ein Kachelofen. Die Bauernmöbel stammen aus der Gegend. Die traditionellen Masken aus Holz trägt man in Bayern beim Straßenfasching. Vor den Fenstern Vorhänge aus altem Leinen. An dem großen Bauerntisch treffen sich Barbara Hammersteins Freunde und deren Freunde zu aufwendigen und phantasievoll inszenierten Mehrgang-Menüs.

Right: The vaulted ceiling of the "Kaminzimmer" – the room with an open hearth – is blackened with soot from the open fire in the old kitchen. Above the fireplace is a wreath of mistletoe which is replaced every New Year.
Below: On the left hand side of the living room is a tiled stove; the rustic furniture was made locally. The traditional wooden masks are worn in the streets in Bavaria during February's Carnival celebrations. The curtains are of antique linen. Barbara Hammerstein's friends and their friends gather around the large rustic table to savour elaborate and imaginative multi-course menus.

A droite: Le plafond voûté de la pièce qui abrite la cheminée est noirci par la suie de l'âtre de l'ancienne cuisine. De grosses boules de gui pendent au-dessus de la cheminée. Chaque année, au premier de l'an, une nouvelle boule de gui est suspendue au plafond.
Ci-dessous: à gauche, dans le séjour, un poêle de faïence; les meubles proviennent tous de la région. Les masques traditionnels en bois sont portés dans la rue lors du «Fasching» (le carnaval bavarois, au mois de février). Aux fenêtres, des rideaux taillés dans de la vieille toile de lin. Autour de cette table paysanne se réunissent les amis de Barbara Hammerstein et leurs propres amis, pour savourer des repas gastronomiques élaborés avec beaucoup de soin et de fantaisie.

Oben: *Blick vom Kaminzimmer in das Bücherzimmer und in den Gewölbegang, der zur Küche führt. Der bemalte Bauernschrank stammt aus dem Jahre 1780.*

Rechts: *Den Mittelpunkt der Küche bildet eine alte Ladentheke. Sie dient als Arbeitsfläche und Vorratsschrank. Auf der anderen Seite befinden sich Dutzende von Schubladen für Reis, Mehl, Kaffee, Zucker und Salz.*

Above: *view from the "Kaminzimmer" into the library and the arched corridor leading to the kitchen. The painted rustic cupboard dates from 1780.*

Right: *In the centre of the kitchen an old shop counter serves as a work surface; on the other side are dozens of drawers, for rice, flour, coffee, sugar and salt.*

Ci-dessus: *vue sur la bibliothèque et le passage cintré. L'armoire rustique peinte date de 1780.*

A droite: *Au milieu de la cuisine, un ancien comptoir de magasin sert de plan de travail; on aperçoit de l'autre côté de multiples tiroirs pour ranger les provisions: riz, farine, café, sucre et sel.*

Although based in Vienna and working for an international clientele, the architect, Professor Wilhelm Holzbauer always longed to own a house in Salzburg, his native city. In 1989, he found the ideal plot of land in the most beautiful part of the city, on the historic boulevard leading to Hellbrunn Castle. Holzbauer had to accept that he was not allowed to alter the external appearance of the makeshift structure standing on the plot, so he needed all his ingenuity to create a home here for himself, his Japanese wife and daughter. Within the small area occupied by the previous building, he constructed a single, multipurpose space the height of a house. The glazed porch with terrace, the glass façade above the entrance and the narrow lancet windows flanking the steep beech and pear wood staircase leading to the gallery all add brightness and result in a dazzling play of light and shade. The elegant, refined furniture is designed down to the last detail by Holzbauer himself.

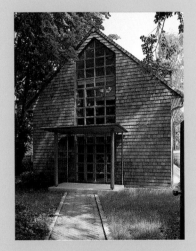

Wilhelm Holzbauer

Professor Wilhelm Holzbauer arbeitet in Wien für eine internationale Klientel. Schon immer hatte der Architekt den Wunsch, ein Haus in seiner Heimatstadt Salzburg zu besitzen. 1989 fand er schließlich ein ideales Grundstück, in der schönsten Gegend der Stadt: an der historischen Allee, die zu Schloß Hellbrunn führt. Holzbauer nahm in Kauf, daß es mit einem Behelfsheim bebaut war, dessen Außenhülle er nicht verändern durfte, und machte für sich, seine japanische Frau und seine Tochter das Beste daraus. Da die Grundfläche relativ klein ist, wurde das Haus zu einem einzigen multifunktionalen, haushohen Raum. Der Glasvorbau mit Terrasse, die Glasfront am Eingang und die schmalen Fensterschlitze entlang der steilen Treppe aus Buche und Birnbaum, die zur Galerie führt, geben dem Gebäude Helligkeit und erlauben verblüffende Licht-Schatten-Spiele. Die feine und edle Einrichtung hat Wilhelm Holzbauer bis ins kleinste Detail selbst ausgewählt.

Il travaille à Vienne et sa clientèle est internationale. Pourtant, l'architecte Wilhelm Holzbauer avait toujours rêvé de posséder une maison dans sa ville natale de Salzbourg. En 1989, il trouve le terrain idéal dans le plus beau quartier de la ville, sur l'allée historique qui mène au château de Hellbrunn. Les dispositions d'urbanisme interdisent de modifier l'aspect extérieur de la maison située dans un secteur sauvegardé mais Holzbauer s'en accommode très bien et tire le meilleur parti de la construction, où il vit désormais avec sa femme et sa fille. La surface de plancher étant réduite, Holzbauer décide de modifier l'intérieur du volume existant: il supprime les différents niveaux et crée à la place un seul espace, ample et multifonctionnel. Sources de clarté, la haute véranda, la verrière de l'entrée ainsi que les minces ouvertures vitrées pratiquées le long du raide escalier en bois de hêtre et de poirier qui dessert la mezzanine, produisent des effets de lumière surprenants. La décoration intérieure, entièrement imaginée par Holzbauer, se distingue par son élégance raffinée.

Vorhergehende Doppelseite, links: Blick vom Eßbereich auf die Felder. An der Terrasse fließt der Hellbrunner Bach vorbei.
Vorhergehende Doppelseite, rechts: Die Schindeln an der Außenwand sind aus Lärchenholz; Blick auf die Sonnenseite des Hauses mit Glasvorbau und Terrasse.
Oben: Das Design der offenen Küche stammt von Paolo Piva.
Rechte Seite: Blick auf die Wand aus Stucco antico, hinter der sich die Treppe zur Schlafgalerie verbirgt. Der Boden ist aus Buchenholz.

Previous pages, left: view across the fields from the dining area of the main room with the Hellbrunn stream flowing past the terrace.
Previous pages, right: The shingles on the outer wall are larch; a view of the sunny side of the house with the glass veranda.
Above: The kitchen which opens out onto the main room was designed by Paolo Piva.
Facing page: The stucco antico wall conceals the staircase to the sleeping quarters on the gallery. The floor is beech wood.

Double page précédente, à gauche: vue sur le paysage environnant depuis le coin repas. La rivière de Hellbrunn coule au pied de la terrasse.
Double page précédente, à droite: Les bardeaux du mur extérieur sont en mélèze; la maison, vue du côté exposé au soleil, avec la terrasse et la véranda.
Ci-dessus: Le design de la cuisinette est de Paolo Piva.
Page de droite: à l'arrière-plan, le mur en stuc à l'ancienne, derrière lequel est dissimulé l'escalier desservant la mezzanine. Le plancher est en hêtre.

Built by the painter Sonja Knapp for herself and her parents in the late Sixties, the chalet stands in an enviable position on the sunny slopes of Klosters. It was in this house that the film diva Greta Garbo found sanctuary in her twilight years. The white walls of the typical Engadine house harmonise beautifully with the 17th- and 18th-century English and Italian furniture, which Sonja Knapp blends with Grisons antiques from the same period, as well as oriental and modern art. Her studio is her favourite room, not least because, after decades as muse and general factotum to French fashion designer Emanuel Ungaro, she has discovered her own passion for painting.

Sonja Knapp

Ihr Chalet liegt am begehrten Sonnenhang von Klosters. Bereits Ende der sechziger Jahre erbaute die Malerin Sonja Knapp für sich und ihre Eltern dieses Domizil, in dem auch die Filmdiva Greta Garbo in den letzten Jahren ihres Lebens ihr Refugium fand. Zu den schlichten weißen Mauern des typischen Engadiner-Hauses passen gut die englischen und italienischen Möbel aus dem 17. und 18. Jahrhundert, die Sonja Knapp mit Graubündner Antiquitäten aus derselben Zeit, Asiatika und moderner Kunst kombiniert. Ihr Lieblingsraum ist das Atelier, wohl auch, weil sie nach Jahrzehnten als Muse an der Seite des französischen Modeschöpfers Emanuel Ungaro entdeckt hat, daß ihre eigentliche Passion die Malerei ist.

Le chalet de Sonja Knapp se dresse sur le versant ensoleillé de Klosters. Bâti pour le peintre et sa famille à la fin des années soixante, il fut aussi le refuge de la grande Greta Garbo à la fin de sa vie. Les murs blancs de cette maison typiquement engadine font ressortir les meubles anglais et italiens des 17e et 18e siècles, que Sonja Knapp marie avec des antiquités grisonnes de la même époque, des objets d'Extrême-Orient et des œuvres d'art moderne. L'atelier est sa pièce préférée depuis qu'elle s'est découvert une passion pour la peinture, après avoir été pendant des années la muse et la collaboratrice du couturier parisien Emanuel Ungaro.

Vorhergehende Doppelseite, links: *Sonja Knapp in ihrem Atelier; Zeichenutensilien.*
Vorhergehende Doppelseite, rechts: *Katzen sind das Hauptmotiv der Künstlerin.*
Linke Seite: *Ansicht des Wohnraums mit Aufgang zu den Fremden- und Schlafzimmern. Links steht ein spanischer Geschirrschrank aus dem 17. Jahrhundert und unter der Treppe eine englische Anrichte von 1750. Im Vordergrund befindet sich ein Graubündner Tisch aus dem 18. Jahrhundert aus Arve, einer Kiefernart.*
Oben: *Das Atelier ist ein ehemaliges Stallgebäude aus Klosters, das Sonja Knapp an ihr Haus anbaute. Das Scheunentor zum Einbringen des Heus ist nun mit einer japanischen Shoji-Papiertür versehen.*
Rechts: *Malutensilien: hier Pinsel aus Japan.*

Previous pages, left: *Sonja Knapp in her studio; drawing utensils.*
Previous pages, right: *Cats are the artist's favourite motif.*
Facing page: *view of the living room with a staircase leading to bedrooms and guest rooms. On the left, a 17th-century Spanish china cupboard, under the staircase an English equivalent of about 1750. In the foreground is an 18th-century Swiss arolla pine table from the Grisons.*
Above: *The studio is a former stable which Sonja Knapp brought from Klosters and built on to her house. The opening where the hay was delivered has been enhanced by a Japanese Shoji paper door.*
Right: *Japanese paintbrushes.*

Double page précédente, à gauche: *Sonja Knapp dans son atelier; matériel de dessin.*
Double page précédente, à droite: *Les chats sont les sujets privilégiés du peintre.*
Page de gauche: *la salle à manger, avec l'escalier accédant aux chambres. A gauche, un buffet espagnol du 17e siècle; sous l'escalier, un bahut anglais de 1750 environ. Au premier plan, une table en pin arolle des Grisons (18e siècle).*
Ci-dessus: *L'atelier est une ancienne étable de Klosters que Sonja Knapp a fait rajouter à la maison. La porte pour engranger le foin est à présent camouflée derrière une porte japonaise en papier Shoji.*
A droite: *matériel de peinture; ici, des pinceaux du Japon.*

Der untere Teil des Stalls dient als Wohn- und Eßzimmer. Die Treppe links führt hinauf ins Atelier. Der toskanische Sakristeischrank stammt aus dem 17. Jahrhundert. Links davon steht ein mit einem Kaschmir bedeckter alter Bündner Tisch aus Davos, rechts ein italienischer Klostertisch, auf dem sich Kerzenhalter aus Brenneisen aus dem 18. Jahrhundert befinden.

The lower part of the stable serves as a living and dining room, with the staircase on the left leading up to the studio. The Tuscan sacristy cupboard dates from the 17th century, while the table on the left, covered by a cashmere cloth, is a Grisons antique from Davos. Standing on the Italian refectory table are 18th-century candlesticks made from branding irons.

Le premier niveau de l'étable sert à la fois de salon et de salle à manger. A gauche, l'escalier conduit à l'étage où se trouve l'atelier. Le meuble de sacristie toscan date du 17e siècle; à gauche, une vieille table de Davos nappée d'une pièce de cachemire; à droite, une table de monastère italienne portant des bougeoirs réalisés à partir de fers à marquer du 18e siècle.

Der Wohnraum des Hauses: Sofa und Sessel stammen aus England und sind mit alten Kaschmirstoffen bedeckt. Auf dem niedrigen Tisch aus Siam steht eine Skulptur aus Granit und Stahl von Pascal Knapp, Sonja Knapps Neffen. Die Fenster links schmücken japanische Sudare und rechts bündnerische Butzenscheiben. Die Vorhänge sind Originale von Fortuny aus Venedig. Alte Kelims bedecken den Parkettboden. Neben dem französischen Geschirrschrank steht ein langer Drapiertisch aus Paris. Rechts hängen zwei Arbeiten von Pablo Picasso.

The sofa and armchairs in the living room are English and covered with old cashmere fabric. The low table is from Siam; the granite and steel sculpture is the work of Sonja's nephew Pascal Knapp. The windows on the left are fitted with Japanese sudare, those on the right with decorative "Butzenscheiben", or bull's-eye panes typical of the Grisons. The curtains are original Fortunys from Venice and the kelims on the floor are antique. Next to the French china cabinet is a long draper's work table from Paris. The paintings on the right are by Pablo Picasso.

Dans le salon, le canapé et les fauteuils anglais sont recouverts de cachemires anciens; la table basse vient du Siam, la sculpture en granit et en acier est l'œuvre de Pascal Knapp, neveu du peintre. Les fenêtres de gauche sont garnies de sudare japonais, celles de droite, «Butzenscheiben», de vitres typiquement grisonnes, en culs de bouteilles. Les rideaux sont de véritable Fortuny de Venise, les tapis, de très vieux kilims. Le vaisselier français est flanqué d'une longue table à draper de Paris. A droite, deux œuvres de Pablo Picasso.

The objects and furniture designed by Freya Krummel are simple, fas-
cinating and practical. Examples include a writing desk which also
functions as a lamp and a folding chair with a foot rest. Born in
Berlin, she studied sculpture at Vienna's Academy of Fine Arts, where
she took master classes with Fritz Wotruba, later spending six years in
Los Angeles where she worked as an interior designer. She and her
husband found a home of their own in 1986, the Flamhof in Styria.
The baroque villa was rebuilt between 1730 and 1750, but a building
was first recorded on the site in 1350. Its total of 28 rooms are spread
over three floors, and from the park there are views as far as Slovenia.
The climate is mild and the house has a bright, Southern atmosphere. Freya and Franz Krummel enjoy buying new things for the
house and rearranging what is already there.

Freya und
Franz Krummel

Freya Krummel entwirft Objekte und Möbel, die geradlinig, außer-
gewöhnlich und praktisch sind: einen Schreibtisch zum Beispiel,
der gleichzeitig Beleuchtungsobjekt ist, oder einen Klappstuhl mit
Fußstütze. Die in Berlin geborene Designerin studierte zunächst
Bildhauerei in der Meisterklasse von Fritz Wotruba an der Akade-
mie der Bildenden Künste in Wien. Anschließend ging sie für sechs
Jahre nach Los Angeles, wo sie als Innenarchitektin arbeitete. Ihr
Zuhause fanden sie und ihr Mann 1986 in der Steiermark im Flamhof. Die Villa wurde zwischen 1730 und 1750 umgebaut, aber schon
1350 erstmals urkundlich erwähnt. Die insgesamt 28 Zimmer verteilen sich auf drei Etagen. Vom Park aus reicht der Blick bis nach
Slowenien. Das Klima ist mild und die Stimmung im Haus leicht
und südlich. Der Flamhof verändert sich ständig. Interessantes
wird dazugekauft und Vorhandenes Änderungen unterworfen.

Les meubles et les objets que crée Freya Krummel sont limpides et
utilitaires, et par là intéressants: un bureau, par exemple, est en même
temps un bel objet d'éclairage, un repose-pied agrémente une simple
chaise pliante. Née à Berlin, Freya Krummel a étudié la sculpture
dans la classe de Fritz Wotruba à l'Académie des beaux-arts de Vienne
puis a travaillé pendant six ans à Los Angeles comme architecte
d'intérieur. C'est en 1986, au Flamhof, en Styrie, que son mari et elle
ont trouvé leur véritable chez-soi. La villa, mentionnée dès 1350 dans
un document d'archives, fut réaménagée entre 1730 et 1750. Les
28 pièces sont réparties sur trois étages, et du parc, la vue s'étend
jusqu'en Slovénie. Le climat est doux et, à l'intérieur, l'atmosphère est
d'une légèreté méridionale. La maison, lumineuse, se transforme sans
cesse: des objets intéressants viennent s'y ajouter et ce qui existe déjà
est souvent modifié. Freya et Franz Krummel aiment déplacer les
meubles, poser les tapis dans d'autres pièces ou installer un objet
d'art devant un autre mur.

Eingangsseiten, links: *Die Stuckdecke, Türen und Beschläge im Salon stammen aus dem Barock.*
Eingangsseiten, rechts: *Villa Flamhof.*
Vorhergehende Doppelseite: *Blick vom Salon in die Bibliothek. Der Teppich ist eine türkische Zeltbahn aus dem 18. Jahrhundert, der Barschrank Art déco. Das Gemälde schuf Albert Oehlen. Der Barockofen ist von außen zu beheizen.*
Oben: *Blick vom Badezimmer in den Salon. Ein Kasak aus dem 19. Jahrhundert dient als Teppich. Schrank und Telefontischchen stammen aus der Zeit des Biedermeiers.*
Rechts: *Blick vom Schlafzimmer ins Badezimmer. Der Druck rechts stammt von Henri Laurens, die Bilder im Bad schuf Hubert Kiecol. Die Etagère hat Freya Krummel entworfen.*

First pages, left: *Stucco ceilings in the drawing room; doors and ornamental mountings stem from the baroque era.*
First pages, right: *Villa Flamhof.*
Previous pages: *the library seen from the drawing room. The rug is an 18th-century Turkish canvas strip, the bar an Art deco cupboard. The painting is by Albert Oehlen. The baroque stove is heated up from outside the room.*
Above: *the drawing room seen from the bathroom. The carpet is a 19th-century Kazakh, the cabinet and telephone table are Biedermeier.*
Right: *the bathroom seen from the bedroom; the print on the right is by Henri Laurens, the pictures beside the bath are by Hubert Kiecol. Etagère by Freya Krummel.*

Premières pages, à gauche: *Les moulages en stuc du plafond, les portes et les ferrures sont baroques.*
Premières pages, à droite: *la villa Flamhof vue depuis la cour intérieure et le parc.*
Double page précédente: *le salon, avec vue sur la bibliothèque. Le tapis est une toile de tente turque du 18e siècle; le bar est de style Art déco. Le grand tableau au mur a été réalisé par Albert Oehlen. Le poêle baroque se chauffe de l'extérieur.*
Ci-dessus: *vue du salon depuis la salle de bain. Le tapis originaire de Kazakhie date du 19e siècle. L'armoire et la petite table de téléphone sont Biedermeier.*
A droite: *la salle de bain vue depuis la chambre. Le tableau, à droite, est de Henri Laurens, ceux de la salle de bain, de Hubert Kiecol. Le meuble à étagères est une création de Freya Krummel.*

Rechts: Detailansicht der Gästetoilette. Der Spiegel und die Etagère stammen aus der Zeit des Art déco. Die Bilder schuf Sigmar Polke.
Unten: Blick von der Küche ins Eßzimmer. Das Gemälde rechts stammt von Arnulf Rainer. Die Einrichtung umfaßt Jugendstil-Anrichten und von Freya Krummel entworfene Stühle.

Right: detail of the guest bathroom. The mirror and étagère are Art deco. Paintings by Sigmar Polke.
Below: view of the kitchen from the dining room, picture on the right by Arnulf Rainer. The sideboards are Art Nouveau, the chairs designed by Freya Krummel.

A droite: Dans cette petite pièce réservée aux invités, le miroir et les étagères sont de style Art déco, les tableaux, de Sigmar Polke.
Ci-dessous: la salle à manger vue depuis la cuisine. Le tableau, à droite, est de Arnulf Rainer. Les dressoirs sont Art nouveau, les chaises, une création de Freya Krummel.

The magnificent "Maihof", in the canton of Schwyz, is surrounded by lush meadows and ancient trees. Built at the end of the 17th century by a general in the service of the Hapsburg Emperor, the fortress-like palace has belonged to the family of an agricultural engineer and international electoral scrutineer since 1916. Three lively children, guinea pigs, cats and dogs ensure that a happy family atmosphere reigns in this stately mansion, preserved in purest Italian baroque style. The estate covers four hectares of land and half a hectare of garden, both as carefully maintained as the house itself with its antiques, paintings and fittings. Maihof is under constant restoration and renovation, since the family hope to live here for many more generations.

Maihof

Umgeben von satten Wiesen und uralten Bäumen steht der prachtvolle »Maihof« inmitten der Schwyzer Landschaft. Gegen Ende des 17. Jahrhunderts von einem General in kaiserlich habsburgischen Diensten erbaut, gehört das burgartige Palais seit 1916 der Familie eines Agraringenieurs und internationalen Wahlbeobachters. Drei ausgelassene Kinder sowie Meerschweinchen, Katzen und Hunde sorgen für einen fröhlichen Familienalltag im italienischen Barock-Ambiente. Vier Hektar Liegenschaft und ein halber Hektar Garten werden ebenso sorgfältig gepflegt wie das Haus selbst. Seine Antiquitäten, Gemälde und Einbauten werden ständiger Restaurierung und Renovierung unterzogen. Der Maihof soll schließlich noch vielen Generationen als Wohnsitz dienen.

La magnifique demeure de «Maihof» se trouve en pleine campagne suisse, au milieu de prés foisonnants et de vieux arbres. Cette résidence aux allures de château fort a été bâtie au 17e siècle par un général aux ordres du Habsbourg. Elle appartient depuis 1916 à la famille d'un ingénieur agronome, observateur électoral de surcroît. Trois enfants exubérants, des cochons d'Inde, des chats, des chiens mettent de la vie dans ce manoir du plus pur style baroque italien. Les quatre hectares du domaine et le demi-hectare de jardin sont parfaitement entretenus, tout comme la maison qui, avec ses antiquités, sa collection de tableaux et ses embellissements, est constamment restaurée et rénovée: de nombreuses générations pourront ainsi encore se succéder à Maihof.

Vorhergehende Doppelseite, links: Außenansicht des Maihofs von Süden aus; der Natursteinweg weist durch das Südtor in die Schwyzer Landschaft.
Vorhergehende Doppelseite, rechts: der anderthalbgeschossige Festsaal im ersten Stock mit der 3,75 Meter hohen Bibliothek.
Oben: ledergebundene antike Bücher.
Rechts: Der Festsaal beherbergt die Bibliothek des Maihofs. Er ist wie das gesamte Anwesen in reinstem italienischem Barock ausgestattet und dient dem heutigen Hausherrn und seiner Familie als Wohnraum.

Previous pages, left: view of Maihof from the south; the stone driveway leads through the south gate into the Schwyz countryside.
Previous pages, right: the one-and-a-half-storey ballroom on the first floor with 3.75 metre-high bookcases.
Above: Leather-bound antiquarian books.
Right: The ballroom houses the Maihof library, which, like the entire estate, is purest Italian baroque and now serves as a living room for the present owner and his family.

Double page précédente, à gauche: une vue extérieure du domaine de «Maihof»; le chemin de pierre qui mène du portail sud à la campagne environnante.
Double page précédente, à droite: la salle de réception du premier étage avec sa galerie et sa bibliothèque de 3,75 mètres de haut.
Ci-dessus: livres anciens reliés en cuir.
A droite: La salle de réception qui abrite la bibliothèque est, comme le reste de la maison, en pur baroque italien. Elle sert de salle de séjour aux propriétaires actuels.

Durch eine zweiflüglige Eichentür gelangt man in die große Eingangshalle. Der Kiesboden des Innenhofs geht in Sandstein über.
Die Truhen stammen aus dem ausgehenden 17. Jahrhundert.

An oak double door leads into the large entrance hall; its sandstone
floor extends out into the gravelled inner courtyard. The chests date
from the end of the 17th century.

Une porte à deux battants en chêne ouvre sur le grand vestibule.
Le sol en grès déborde sur la cour intérieure tapissée de graviers.
Les coffres datent de la fin du 17e siècle.

Das Parkett und die Möbel im Salon im Erdgeschoß sind wie die Ausstattung des gesamten Palais im Laufe der Jahre sorgfältig restauriert worden.

The floor and furniture in the ground-floor drawing room, as in the entire palace, have been painstakingly restored over the course of the years.

Comme le reste de la propriété, le parquet et les meubles du salon du rez-de-chaussée ont été soigneusement restaurés au cours des ans.

"Frau Ingrid", the "flower lady" was everybody's darling. Her stunningly beautiful bouquets, her own silk flowers, every bloom a work of art, and her sumptuous floral arrangements recalled the still-life paintings of the Old Masters. Flowers from Ingrid Mayerhofer's "Blumenstube", which has been owned, since her death, by her son Alexander, adorn the homes of native Salzburgers and the distinguished summer visitors who flock to the city for the Festival. With her highly-developed sense of beauty, Ingrid Mayerhofer provided the decorations for the wedding feast of the Prince and Princess von Thurn und Taxis at their palace in Regensburg as well as for many other grand celebrations held by Germany and Austria's rich and famous. Her son Alexander finds tranquillity and inspiration in the 300-year-old house, a farmhouse in the traditional style of the Flachgau region, 25 kilometres north of Salzburg, near Lake Mattsee. Generations of farmers once grazed their cattle here; then the cows gave way to beds of beautiful flowers, later destined to warm the hearts of others.

Alexander Mayerhofer

Alle liebten »Frau Ingrid« und ihre Blumen. Ingrid Mayerhofer war berühmt für ihre wunderschönen frischen Sträuße, vor allem aber für ihre üppigen Seidenblumengestecke, die an die Stilleben Alter Meister erinnern. Blumen aus Mayerhofers »Blumenstube«, die ihr Sohn Alexander nach ihrem Tod fortführt, verschönern die Häuser der Salzburger und der prominenten Sommergäste, die zu den Festspielen in die Stadt kommen. Ingrid Mayerhofer hat das Regensburger Schloß für die Hochzeitsgala des Fürstenpaares von Thurn und Taxis geschmückt und manch anderes großes Fest deutscher und österreichischer Prominenz mit feinem Sinn für das Schöne ausgestattet. Ruhe und Inspiration findet nun der Sohn in dem 25 Kilometer nördlich von Salzburg gelegenen, 300 Jahre alten, typischen Flachgauhaus in der Nähe des Mattsees. Generationen von Bauern hatten dort ihr Vieh gezüchtet, heute gedeihen hier prachtvolle Blumen, die später anderer Leute Herzen erfreuen.

Tout le monde aimait «Madame Ingrid» et ses fleurs. Elle confectionnait des bouquets de fleurs fraîches, mais surtout de fleurs artificielles en soie, véritables œuvres d'art, opulentes compositions florales qui rappellent les natures mortes des grands maîtres de la peinture. Les bouquets de la «Blumenstube» («chambre des fleurs»), que perpétue Alexander Mayerhofer après la mort de sa mère, fleurissent les demeures salzbourgeoises et les résidences des personnalités venues assister au festival de Salzbourg. Ingrid Mayerhofer a réalisé la décoration florale du gala donné pour les noces du couple princier Thurn und Taxis au château de Ratisbonne et fleuri aussi avec un goût très sûr maintes fêtes organisées par des célébrités allemandes et autrichiennes. C'est dans sa maison située à proximité du lac de Mattsee, à 25 kilomètres de Salzbourg, qu'Alexander Mayerhofer trouve le calme et l'inspiration. La vieille ferme a été construite il y a 300 ans dans le style typique de la région du Flachgau. Dans cette maison où, pendant des générations, des paysans ont élevé du bétail, poussent aujourd'hui des fleurs dont la beauté fait la joie de leurs acquéreurs.

Linke Seite: *Hauseingang; das Mayerhofersche Flachgauhaus mit den typischen Holzschindeln.*
Oben: *Von dem Balkon aus überblickt man den Garten. Vor dem Haus stehen inmitten des satten Grüns Tisch und Bänke aus weißem Marmor.*

Facing page: *the entrance; the Flachgau house with its typical wooden shingles.*
Above: *The balcony overlooks the garden; a white marble table and benches amid the lush green of the garden.*

Page de gauche: *l'entrée de la maison; la maison, avec ses bardeaux en bois caractéristiques. Le balcon donne sur le jardin.*
Ci-dessus: *Devant la maison, le marbre blanc de la table et des bancs contraste avec le vert saturé de la pelouse.*

Linke Seite: *Neben dem Kamin im großen Wohnzimmer finden sich prachtvolle Beispiele von Ingrid und Alexander Mayerhofers Blumenkunst.*
Oben: *Im oberen Geschoß, in der ehemaligen Tenne, befindet sich ein großzügiges offenes Wohnstudio.*
Rechts: *Naive Bilder mit bäuerlichen Szenen und Werke der Volkskunst schmücken Wände und Nischen.*

Facing page: *The fireplace in the large living room is surrounded by splendid examples of Ingrid and Alexander Mayerhofer's floral art.*
Above: *Upstairs, the former threshing floor has been transformed into a spacious living area.*
Right: *Walls and niches are enhanced by folk art and naive paintings of rustic scenes.*

Page de gauche: *La cheminée de la grande salle de séjour est encadrée par de splendides créations florales d'Ingrid et Alexander Mayerhofer.*
Ci-dessus: *A l'étage supérieur, l'ancienne aire de battage a été transformée en salon spacieux.*
A droite: *Murs et niches sont mis en valeur par des objets d'art traditionnel et par des peintures naïves de scènes rustiques.*

Links: *Kruzifix und Rosenkränze.*
Rechts: *eine holzgeschnitzte Kuh.*

Left: *crucifix and rosaries.*
Right: *carved wooden cow.*

A gauche: *un crucifix et des rosaires.*
A droite: *une vache en bois sculptée.*

Rechts: *eine Sammlung von Monstranzen und Marienfiguren.*

Right: *collection of monstrances and statues of the Virgin Mary.*

A droite: *une collection d'ostensoirs et de madones.*

Rechte Seite: *Das von Lockvögeln aus Holz umrahmte antike Flachgauer Bauernbett ist mit Blumenornamenten und Heiligenbildern bemalt.*

Facing page: *Framed by wooden decoy birds, the antique Flachgau rustic bed is painted with floral and religious motifs.*

Page de droite: *Le vieux lit, bien dans le style du Flachgau, est encadré d'appeaux en bois; les montants sont peints de motifs magnifiques.*

Links: *Stilleben mit Wiege.*
Rechts: *Lampenmaske der Salzburger Volkskunst.*

Left: *still life with cradle.*
Right: *carved lamp screens typical of the Salzburg region.*

A gauche: *berceau agrémenté d'une nature morte.*
A droite: *écran de lampe représentatif de l'art populaire salzbourgeois.*

Above the entrance of Juval Fortress are the words "Tashi delek", Tibetan for "happiness and peace". The 13th-century fortress, rebuilt between 1542 and 1548, is in the Vintschgau valley in South Tyrol, near the little village of Staben, and is home to globe-trotting Reinhold Messner: mountaineer, author and documentary film-maker. He was searching for a place where he could gather his thoughts, raise his children, cultivate wine and bake bread, when, in 1983, he found Juval and transformed it in typical Messner style into a blend of Renaissance castle, Tibetan monastery and South Tyrolean village. Part of the fortress is open to the public, and the complex includes seven working farms and three guest houses. Today, there are 23 children and 100 different breeds of birds living in and around the fortress. Gigantic Tibetan cedars stand in the courtyard, and Messner has laid out a Zen garden among the ruins of the fortified walls.

Reinhold Messner

»Tashi delek« steht über dem Eingang der Burg Juval geschrieben. Das ist tibetisch und bedeutet »Glück und Frieden«. Der Trutzbau aus dem 13. Jahrhundert wurde zwischen 1542 und 1548 umgebaut und liegt im Südtiroler Vintschgau, bei dem Örtchen Staben. Er ist die Heimat des Weltreisenden, Bergsteigers, Autors und Dokumentarfilmers Reinhold Messner. Auf der Suche nach einem Ort der Ruhe, wo er seine Kinder großziehen, Wein anbauen und Brot backen kann, fand er 1983 Burg Juval. Inzwischen hat er die Burg zum typischen Messner-Land umgestaltet: Renaissanceschloß, tibetisches Kloster und Südtiroler Dorf in einem. Teile der Burg kann man besichtigen. Es gibt sieben Gehöfte auf dem Hügel von Juval und drei Gasthäuser. 23 Kinder leben heute in und unweit der Burg, außerdem 100 verschiedene Vogelarten. Im Schloßhof stehen riesige Himalaja-Zedern, und zwischen den zerfallenen Mauern des Burgwalls hat Messner einen Zen-Garten angelegt.

«Tashi delek», peut-on lire au-dessus de l'entrée du château de Juval. En tibétain, cela signifie «bonheur et paix». Cette forteresse, édifiée au 13e siècle et modifiée entre 1542 et 1548, à proximité du village de Staben, sur une hauteur de la vallée du Vintschgau dans le Tyrol du Sud, est la demeure d'un célèbre alpiniste, grand voyageur, écrivain et documentariste de surcroît: Reinhold Messner. A la recherche d'un endroit où il pourrait méditer en paix, élever ses enfants, produire du vin et cuire du pain, il découvre le site en 1983 et en fait quelque chose de typiquement messnérien: un château Renaissance, un couvent tibétain et un village tyrolien tout à la fois. Une partie du château est ouverte au public, et, sur le site, qui comprend aussi sept exploitations agricoles et trois auberges, vivent 23 enfants et une centaine d'espèces d'oiseaux. Messner a planté au beau milieu de la cour du château des gigantesques cèdres de l'Himalaya et, sur un espace entre les murs en ruine du rempart, il a aménagé un jardin zen.

Vorhergehende Doppelseite, links: Reinhold Messner; seine Burg.
Vorhergehende Doppelseite, rechts: Burg Juval thront auf der Bergkante zwischen dem Schnalstal und dem Vintschgau.
Unten: der »Saal der Tausend Freuden« mit Fresken aus der Renaissance. Hier bewirtet Messner gelegentlich Freunde bei fröhlichen Festen.

Previous pages, left: Reinhold Messner; his mountain fortress.
Previous pages, right: The Juval Fortress towers over the mountainside between the Schnals and Vintschgau Valleys.
Below: the "Room of a Thousand Delights" with Renaissance frescos. Messner occasionally holds parties here for friends.

Double page précédente, à gauche: Reinhold Messner; son château.
Double page précédente, à droite: Le château de Juval se dresse audessus d'un abîme, entre deux vallées, le Schnalstal et le Vintschgau.
Ci-dessous: la «Salle des mille joies», ornée de fresques de la Renaissance. C'est la pièce où Messner rassemble ses amis pour de joyeuses fêtes.

Überall in der Burg – wie hier im Wohnzimmer – befinden sich
prachtvolle alte Kachelöfen. In die Keramikkacheln des grünen Ofens
in der Bibliothek sind alle Achttausender eingebrannt, die Messner
bestiegen hat.

There are beautiful old tiled stoves all over the fortress – like this one
in the living room. Each of the 8 000 metre peaks scaled by Messner
is depicted, burned into the ceramic tiles of the green oven on the
right, located in the library.

Un peu partout dans le château, comme ici, dans le séjour, se trouvent de magnifiques poêles de faïence. Sur celui de la bibliothèque,
les carreaux de couleur verte portent l'empreinte de tous les sommets
de 8 000 mètres atteints par Messner au cours de sa carrière.

Oben: unter mittelalterlichem Gewölbe: ein Gebetsraum mit Bronzen und Statuen aus Tibet und Nepal.
Rechts: Im »tantrischen Raum«, der dem Totenkult gewidmet ist, befindet sich eine lange »Danba«, die böse Geister vertreiben soll.
Rechte Seite: Zusammentreffen der Weltreligionen in der christlichen Kapelle, die sich offen an einen Flur im Hauptteil der Burg anschließt.

Above: beneath medieval vaults: a prayer room with bronzes and statues from Tibet and Nepal.
Right: In the "Tantra Room", dedicated to the Cult of the Dead, is a long "danba", intended to drive away evil spirits.
Facing page: World religions meet in the Christian chapel, linked directly to a hallway in the main part of the fortress.

Ci-dessus: sous les voûtes médiévales, la salle de prières, avec des bronzes et des statues rapportés du Tibet et du Népal.
A droite: Dans la «salle tantrique», consacrée au culte des morts, se trouve une longue «danba» censée chasser les esprits malins.
Page de droite: La chapelle ouverte, qui donne sur un couloir, dans le corps principal du château, se veut le carrefour des grandes religions.

Linke Seite: eine Fensternische im großen »Maskenzimmer« mit Sitzen aus Tibet.
Oben: das vier Meter hohe »Maskenzimmer« mit Masken und Tapisserien aus Tibet und Nepal.
Rechts: eine tibetische Skulptur.

Facing page: a quiet corner of the great "Mask Room" with Tibetan seats.
Above: the four-metre-high "Mask Room" with masks and tapestries from Tibet and Nepal.
Right: a Tibetan sculpture.

Page de gauche: une niche dans la grande «Salle des masques», avec des chaises du Tibet.
Ci-dessus: La «Salle des masques», dont le plafond s'élève à quatre mètres de hauteur, abrite de superbes masques et tapisseries du Tibet et du Népal.
A droite: une sculpture tibétaine.

Standing high above the Zoldo Valley in the province of Belluno, with a view of the Pelmo and the Civetta is La Casetta, a romantic manor house built between 1924 and 1925 by Baron Piero Parisi. The present owners, Baron Parisi and his wife, Baroness Franca Mico-Parisi, have a soft spot for this isolated house, even though they come here at holiday times. Franca Mico-Parisi, who also has properties in Milan, Venice and the Chianti region, is particularly fond of the work of the naive sculptor Almerindo Rizzardini (1886–1966), a local artist. Rizzardini continued globetrotting until well into old age in his unending search for new commissions and fresh inspiration. His sculptures lend La Casetta a certain humorous charm.

Baronessa Franca Mico-Parisi

Oberhalb des Valle di Zoldo, in der italienischen Provinz Belluno, liegt La Casetta, ein romantisches Landhaus mit Blick auf den Monte Pelmo und den Monte Civetta. Es wurde 1924/1925 von Baron Piero Parisi erbaut. Die heutigen Besitzer, sein Sohn und dessen Frau Franca Mico-Parisi, haben ein Faible für dieses einsam gelegene Haus, auch wenn sie nur an den Feiertagen hierherkommen. Die besondere Liebe der Baronessa, die weitere Anwesen im Chianti, in Mailand und Venedig unterhält, gilt den Werken des Bildhauers Almerindo Rizzardini (1886–1966). Der ortsansässige naive Künstler war stets auf der Suche nach neuen Eindrücken und reiste bis ins hohe Alter um die Welt. Seine Skulpturen geben La Casetta einen besonderen Charme.

Situé sur les hauteurs de la vallée de Zoldo, dans la province de Belluno, en Vénétie, La Casetta, manoir romantique construit en 1924–1925 par le baron Piero Parisi, offre une vue fort belle sur le Pelmo et la Civetta. Les actuelles propriétaires, le baron Parisi et sa femme, la baronne Franca Mico-Parisi, ont un faible pour cette demeure solitaire, même s'ils n'y viennent que les jours de fête. La baronne, qui possède également des propriétés dans le Chianti, à Milan et à Venise, affectionne les œuvres naïves d'Almerindo Rizzardini (1886–1966), un sculpteur de la région. Ce dernier, toujours en quête de travail et de nouvelles impressions, voyagea dans le monde entier jusqu'à un âge avancé. Ses sculptures confèrent à La Casetta un charme quelque peu bizarre.

Vorhergehende Seite: *Durch die Haustür gelangt man in die alte Stube mit Holzwerk aus dem 16. Jahrhundert.*
Oben: *Blick in das Eßzimmer. Die Wandteller aus Bassano del Grappa in Venetien stammen aus dem 19. Jahrhundert. Auf der Fensterbank stehen Holzskulpturen von Almerindo Rizzardini, die Tischsets sind amerikanisches Patchwork.*
Rechte Seite: *eine gemütliche Ecke in der Küche.*

Previous page: *The front door of the house leads into the old living room. The woodwork is 16th-century.*
Above: *view of the dining room. The 19th-century plates on the wall are from the Venetian town Bassano del Grappa. On the window sill are wooden sculptures by Almerindo Rizzardini; the table linen is American patchwork.*
Facing page: *a cosy corner of the kitchen.*

Page précédente: *L'entrée de la maison mène directement dans le vieux salon. Les lambris sont du 16e siècle.*
Ci-dessus: *la salle à manger. Les assiettes murales de la ville vénétienne Bassano del Grappa datent du 19e siècle. Sur la fenêtre, sont exposées des sculptures en bois d'Almerindo Rizzardini; les sets de table sont en patchwork américain.*
Page de droite: *un coin confortable dans la cuisine.*

Linke Seite: Der massive Aufsatzschrank wurde im Valle di Zoldo im 17. Jahrhundert gefertigt. Auch die runden und ovalen Dosen stammen aus der Gegend. Den Holzpfau schuf Almerindo Rizzardini.
Oben: Das breite Doppelbett mit seinen aufwendigen Schnitzereien stammt aus dem 18. Jahrhundert. Links eine Gebetsbank aus dem 17. Jahrhundert. Der Bettüberwurf ist ein amerikanischer Quilt.
Rechts: über der Holztäfelung im Badezimmer eine Blumentapete von Sanderson.

Facing page: The massive 17th-century sideboard was made in the Valle di Zoldo region. The round and oval jars were made locally; the wooden peacock was carved by Almerindo Rizzardini.
Above: The wide double bed with its beautifully carved headboard dates from the 18th-century. On the left is a 17th-century prayer stool. The bedspread is an American quilt.
Right: floral Sanderson wallpaper above the wood panelling in the bathroom.

Page de gauche: L'imposant bahut a été fabriqué au 17e siècle dans la région de Valle di Zoldo. Les petites boîtes rondes et ovales sont une production locale, le paon en bois, une œuvre du sculpteur Almerindo Rizzardini.
Ci-dessus: Le grand lit à deux places avec son beau montant sculpté est du 18e siècle. A gauche, un prie-Dieu du 17e siècle. Le dessus-de-lit est une courtepointe américaine.
A droite: au-dessus du lambris en bois de la salle de bains, un papier à fleurs de Sanderson.

Morgenstätter Hof, a farm on the Riebelsberg in the Sarentina Alps of South Tyrol, is home to three generations: grandfather Johann Nussbaumer and his wife, who live in the cottage reserved for the retired farmer, their stepson Helmut Oberkalmsteiner, who manages the farm, his wife, and their son and daughter. Everyone, even the daughter who is still at school, shares in the work of running the farm. The setting may look idyllic, but there is no concealing the hard labour involved in cultivating 16 hectares of fields and forest, tending the livestock, milking the cows, grinding flour and baking bread. The farm first appeared in the records around 1300 and was later used as a courthouse where judges dispensed justice. Even the mistress of the house cannot say how many rooms the farmhouse has, for she has never bothered to count them. At Morgenstätter Hof there are more important things to do.

Morgenstätter Hof

Drei Generationen bewohnen den Morgenstätter Hof auf dem Riebelsberg im Südtiroler Sarnthein bei Bozen: Großvater Johann Nussbaumer und seine Frau, die auf dem Altenteil sind, Stiefsohn Helmut Oberkalmsteiner, der das Gehöft mit seiner Frau bewirtschaftet, sowie deren Sohn und Tochter. Bis auf die Tochter, die noch zur Schule geht, packen alle kräftig mit an. Die idyllische Landschaft darf aber nicht darüber hinwegtäuschen, wieviel schwere Arbeit hier tagein, tagaus zu leisten ist. Schließlich wollen 16 Hektar Wiesen und Wald bewirtschaftet werden, das Vieh versorgt, die Milch gemolken, das Mehl gemahlen und das Brot gebacken werden. Der Hof wurde erstmals um 1300 erwähnt. Später wachten hier die Richter über Recht und Gerechtigkeit. Wie viele Zimmer der Hof hat? Diese Frage kann die Hausherrin nicht beantworten, gezählt hat sie sie nie. Auf dem Morgenstätter Hof gibt es Wichtigeres zu tun.

La ferme de Morgenstätt, située sur le Riebelsberg, à Sarnthein, près de Bolzano (Tyrol du Sud), est la demeure de trois générations: les grands-parents, Johann Nussbaumer et sa femme, le beau-fils Helmut Oberkalmsteiner et sa femme ainsi que leurs deux enfants, un fils et une fille. Helmut Oberkalmsteiner gère l'exploitation mais tous, hormis sa fille qui va encore à l'école, lui prêtent main-forte. Si le paysage environnant est idyllique, il ne peut toutefois faire oublier que le travail à la ferme est un rude labeur. Seize hectares de prés et de forêt demandent jour après jour à être exploités, le bétail à être nourri, le lait à être trait, le grain à être moulu et le pain à être cuit. L'histoire de la ferme remonte loin dans le temps. Elle est mentionnée pour la première fois en 1300; plus tard, ce fut un tribunal où les juges veillaient au droit et à la justice. Combien de pièces y a-t-il dans la ferme? La maîtresse des lieux est bien incapable de répondre à cette question: elle ne les a jamais comptées. Il est vrai qu'à Morgenstätt, on a plus important à faire.

Eingangsseiten, links: in der Mühle.
Eingangsseiten, rechts: Johann Nussbaumer, der Bauer; an der Decke der Wohnstube schwebt der Heilige Geist als holzgeschnitzte Taube.
Vorhergehende Doppelseite: Blick auf Wiesen und Pferdekoppel.
Oben: Johann Nussbaumer und seine Frau bei der Mahlzeit mit Magd und Knecht.
Rechts: Die taubstumme Magd arbeitet seit ihrer Jugend auf dem Hof. Hier seiht sie die frischgemolkene Milch durch ein Tuch in einen Eimer.

First pages, left: detail of the mill.
First pages, right: the farmer Johann Nussbaumer; the Holy Spirit in the form of a carved wooden dove hovers above the living room.
Previous pages: view of the fields and the paddock.
Above: Johann Nussbaumer and his wife share a meal with the dairy maid and the farm boy.
Right: The dairy maid, a deaf mute who has worked at the farm since her youth, is seen here straining fresh milk into a pail.

Premières pages, à gauche: vue partielle du moulin.
Premières pages, à droite: Johann Nussbaumer. Sous le plafond de la salle de séjour, plane une colombe en bois sculpté figurant l'Esprit saint.
Double page précédente: les prés environnants et le parc à chevaux.
Ci-dessus: Johann Nussbaumer et sa femme en compagnie de la servante et du valet de ferme.
A droite: La servante sourde-muette travaille depuis son jeune âge à la ferme. Ici, elle est en train de filtrer du lait fraîchement tiré dans un seau.

Rechts: Jagdtrophäe aus dem eigenen Wald. In der Wohnstube dienen Rundofen und Bank zum Aufwärmen.
Unten: Das mit Kümmel und Koriander gewürzte Brot lagert in hölzernen Brotrahmen. Es wird – wie fast alles, was auf dem Morgenstätter Hof auf den Tisch kommt – selbst hergestellt. Die Bäuerin backt zweimal im Jahr und trocknet den Vorrat.

Right: a hunting trophy from the farm's own woodland. The bench by the stove provides a warm and cosy place to sit.
Below: Bread, flavoured with caraway and coriander, is kept on wooden shelves. Like almost everything else which appears on the table at Morgenstätter Hof, the bread is home-made. The farmer's wife bakes twice a year and dries the loaves to preserve them.

A droite: Dans la salle de séjour, le trophée est une tête de cerf abattu dans les bois du domaine. Le poêle rond et le banc sont très appréciés les jours de froid.
Ci-dessous: Le pain à la coriandre et au cumin est entreposé sur des rayons en bois. Tout (ou presque) ce qui est consommé à table est fabriqué sur place. Le pain est cuit deux fois par an et conservé par séchage.

Oben: *das Elternschlafzimmer mit Kinderbettchen. Geheizt wird mit dem Ofen.*
Rechte Seite: *die sogenannte »Richterstube« mit Kassettendecke. Wo in vergangenen Jahrhunderten Recht gesprochen wurde, spinnt heute die Bäuerin die Wolle der hofeigenen Schafe. In der Ecke der typisch Tiroler Herrgottswinkel mit Kruzifix.*

Above: *the parents' bedroom with children's cots. Heating is provided by a stove.*
Facing page: *the so-called "Judges' Room" with coffered ceiling. Where once judges dispensed justice, the farmer's wife now spins wool from the farm's own sheep. The room has a typical Tyrolean "Herrgottswinkel" — a corner with a crucifix.*

Ci-dessus: *la chambre des parents, avec un petit lit d'enfant. La pièce est chauffée par un poêle.*
Page de droite: *la «salle des juges» avec son plafond à caissons. C'est ici que fut rendue la justice aux siècles passés. La maîtresse de maison y file maintenant la laine de ses moutons. Le «coin du bon Dieu», typiquement tyrolien avec son crucifix, est placé dans une encoignure de la pièce.*

Oben: Blick auf das Plumpsklo, das bis weit in die siebziger Jahre benutzt wurde.
Rechte Seite: der Altar mit Aufsatz in der Hauskapelle. Die nach der Heiligen Anna benannte Kapelle wurde im 16. Jahrhundert erbaut. Wände und Gewölbe sind reich ausgemalt. Alle zwei Monate liest der Pfarrer aus dem benachbarten Ort eine Messe für die Einödbauern der Umgebung.

Above: view of the earth closet used until the Seventies.
Facing page: the altar of the private chapel. Dedicated to St. Anne, it is believed to have been built in the 16th century. The walls and vaulted ceiling are richly painted. Every two months the priest from the nearby village conducts a service for people living on remote farms in the neighbourhood.

Ci-dessus: vue sur les toilettes rudimentaires utilisées jusque dans les années soixante-dix.
Page de droite: le retable de la chapelle privée construite au 16e siècle et baptisée du nom de sainte Anne. Les murs et les voûtes sont décorés de riches peintures. Tous les deux mois, le curé de la paroisse voisine vient y dire la messe pour les habitants des fermes isolées.

Peter Notz's children are called Cédric and Clarina, which is why he gave his chalet in Gstaad the charming name of "Cédrina". The immaculate house stands in a very sunny and peaceful position in a park-like garden, stocked with old trees. It is only three minutes away from the centre of the village, close to the Palace Hotel, and has views over the Diablerets Glacier, Windspielen and Eggli. Originally a cheese factory built in the nearby valley of Diemtigtal at the end of the 17th century, the building is under a preservation order. In the period between 1988 and 1990, it had to be dismantled, but was lovingly reconstructed in Gstaad, with close attention to materials and details. The layout was adapted to suit the needs of the occupants, a couple with two children and a constant flow of visitors. The old larch woodwork is an example of the carpenter's art at its finest. It is amazing how the elegant 18th-century French furniture harmonises with the rustic style of the building.

Peter Notz

Seine Kinder heißen Cédric und Clarina. Und so gab Peter Notz seinem Chalet in Gstaad den schönen Namen »Cédrina«. Das schmucke Anwesen liegt sehr sonnig und sehr ruhig in einem parkähnlichen Garten mit altem Baumbestand, nur drei Minuten vom Dorfkern entfernt in der Nähe des Hotels Palace. Der Blick geht hinaus auf die Diableretsgletscher, Windspielen und Eggli. Ursprünglich stand das im 17. Jahrhundert erbaute und heute denkmalgeschützte Chalet im benachbarten Diemtigtal und diente als Käserei. Von 1988 bis 1990 mußte es dort abgetragen werden, und wurde schließlich in Gstaad mit viel Liebe zum Detail wieder aufgebaut. Der Grundriß wurde allerdings den Bedürfnissen der Bewohner angepaßt, einer Familie mit zwei Kindern und stets vielen Hausgästen. Die alten Holzarbeiten aus Lärche sind Zeugnisse bester Zimmermannskunst. Verblüffend ist, wie harmonisch sich die eleganten französischen Möbel aus dem 18. Jahrhundert mit dem rustikalen Baustil vertragen.

Peter Notz a baptisé son chalet du joli nom de «Cédrina», d'après les prénoms de ses deux enfants Cédric et Clarina. Cette belle demeure est construite sur un site ensoleillé et calme, à trois minutes seulement du centre de Gstaad, non loin de l'hôtel Palace. Le jardin a des allures de parc avec son peuplement d'arbres très anciens. La vue donne sur les glaciers des Diablerets, sur Windspielen et Eggli. Ce chalet classé monument historique est une ancienne fromagerie de la vallée voisine du Diemtigtal, datant de la fin du 17e siècle, qu'il a fallu démonter et transporter sur le nouveau site. Sa reconstruction a été menée de 1988 à 1990 avec le plus grand soin. Le plan initial a été adapté aux besoins de ses occupants, un couple et ses deux enfants, et de ses nombreux hôtes. Les lambris en mélèze témoignent du meilleur savoir-faire artisanal. L'harmonieux mariage entre les élégants meubles français du 18e siècle et le style rustique du chalet ne laisse pas de surprendre.

Linke Seite: Der Industrielle Peter Notz pendelt zwischen London und Gstaad; Chalet Cédrina war ursprünglich eine Käserei aus dem 17. Jahrhundert.
Oben: Blick vom Salon in das Speisezimmer. Ganz bewußt hat Peter Notz auf eine bäuerliche Einrichtung verzichtet und französische Antiquitäten des 18. Jahrhunderts gewählt. So entsteht ein reizvoller Kontrast.
Folgende Doppelseite: Vom großzügigen Eingangsbereich führt eine Treppe ins Erd- und Dachgeschoß hinauf. Der französische Spiegel stammt aus dem 18. Jahrhundert. Den Bodenbelag bilden alte Steinplatten aus Burgund.

Facing page: Peter Notz is an industrialist who commutes between London and Gstaad; Chalet Cédrina was originally a 17th-century cheese factory.
Above: View of the dining room from the drawing room. Deliberately rejecting a rustic style of furnishing, Peter Notz has chosen French 18th-century antiques, creating a delightful contrast.
Following pages: A staircase leads from the spacious entrance hall up to the ground floor and attic. The mirror is 18th-century French, the antique stone floor is from Burgundy.

Page de gauche: Peter Notz est un industriel qui vit entre Londres et Gstaad; La Cédrina est une ancienne fromagerie du 17e siècle.
Ci-dessus: La salle à manger vue du salon. C'est à dessein que Peter Notz a choisi des antiquités françaises du 18e siècle, de préférence à un ameublement rustique, créant ainsi un contraste des plus intéressants.
Double page suivante: L'escalier de la vaste entrée mène au rez-de-chaussée et à l'étage mansardé. Le miroir français date du 18e siècle. Le vieux dallage est originaire de Bourgogne.

Der Grundriß des ursprünglichen Hauses wurde zugunsten größerer
Zimmer verändert. So legte man auch mehrere Räume für den
großen Salon zusammen.

The original ground plan was opened up to provide more generous
spaces, the large drawing room was created by knocking through
several smaller rooms.

Le grand salon est né de la réunion de plusieurs pièces; le plan initial
du chalet a fait place à une suite de pièces plus spacieuses.

Oben: Detail des großen Salons, von einem anderen Blickwinkel aus gesehen.
Folgende Seite: Blick vom Kaminzimmer in das mit bäuerlichem Mobiliar eingerichtete Büro.

Above: detail of the large drawing room, seen from a different angle.
Following page: view from the "Kaminzimmer" – the room with a fireplace – to the rustically furnished office.

Ci-dessus: détail du grand salon, vu sous un angle différent.
Page suivante: une vue du bureau avec son mobilier rustique depuis la pièce abritant la cheminée.

Links: ein prachtvoller französischer Konsoltisch und ein vergoldeter Spiegel im Speisezimmer.

Left: sumptuous French console and gilded mirror in the dining room.

A gauche: la magnifique console française et le miroir doré de la salle à manger.

Rechts: Überall im Haus, wie hier im Aufgang zum Dachgeschoß, sorgen versteckte Lichtquellen für eine warme Beleuchtung.

Right: All over the house, concealed spots generate a warm light, as here on the staircase to the attic.

A droite: Partout dans la maison, comme c'est le cas ici dans l'escalier qui desssert l'étage mansardé, des spots habilement dissimulés dispensent une chaude lumière.

Rechts: Porzellanfiguren und Lüster aus Bergkristall stehen auf einer Anrichte im Speisezimmer.

Right: Porcelain figures and rock crystal candlesticks are displayed on a dresser in the dining room.

A droite: Des figurines en porcelaine et un chandelier en cristal de roche ornent le bahut de la salle à manger.

Unten: In einem der Schlafzimmer befindet sich ein Bett mit schwerem rotem Damast und vergoldetem Kopfteil.

Below: gilded headboard of a bed upholstered in heavy red damask.

Ci-dessous: dans une des chambres, un montant de lit doré et un couvre-lit en lourd damas de couleur rouge.

Links: oberer Teil der »Kaminhutte«, dem hölzernen Dach des großen zentralen Kamins.

Left: top of the wooden "Kaminhutte", the chimney hood above the central fireplace.

A gauche: la partie supérieure de la «Kaminhutte», la hotte en bois de la grande cheminée centrale.

Der Blick aus dem Schlafzimmer des Hausherrn zeigt, wie perfekt
sich die Farben der Natur in der Bemalung der antiken Kommode
und des Spiegels sowie in den alten Stoffbezügen von Sessel und Bett
wiederholen.

The view from the master bedroom shows how perfectly the colours of
nature are repeated in the paintwork on the antique dressing table
and the mirror, and in the antique fabric used for the armchair uphol-
stery and bedspread.

La chambre du maître de maison: la peinture de la commode ancienne et du miroir ainsi que les vieilles étoffes recouvrant le fauteuil
et le lit reproduisent de manière parfaite les couleurs de la nature.

Alpen Interieurs   Peter Notz

Auch im roten Schlafzimmer der Hausherrin befinden sich französische Möbel und Gemälde aus dem 18. Jahrhundert. Zu jedem Schlafzimmer gehört ein Ankleidezimmer und ein komfortables Marmorbad.

The eighteenth-century French furniture and painting lend a fragile elegance to the red bedroom of the mistress of the house. Each bedroom has its own dressing room and luxurious marble bathroom.

La chambre rouge de la maîtresse de maison se distingue par sa délicate élégance. Elle aussi est garnie de meubles français et de tableaux du 18e siècle. Chacune des chambres dispose d'une salle de bains en marbre et d'un vestiaire.

The Nutli Hüschi house is one of the oldest buildings in the Grisons. Standing in the village of Klosters on the way to the restaurant "Alpenrösli", it was built in 1565 by the Nutlis, a farming family who cultivated the surrounding land. Constructed in typical Prättigau Valley style with square planed timbers, the farm house was allowed to fall into ruin over the centuries, until in 1918 it was bought by Dr Fritz Schoellhorn of Winterthur and lovingly restored and maintained. In 1953, Dr Schoellhorn donated the building to the community. Since then, the Nutli Hüschi house has been open to the public as an outstanding example of a rural home. The basement kitchen leads into the square living room with small windows. There is a bedroom and even a loom on the upper floor.

Nutli Hüschi

Das Nutli Hüschi ist eines der ältesten Häuser Graubündens und liegt im Dorf Klosters auf dem Weg zum Aussichtsrestaurant »Alpenrösli«. 1565 wurde es von der Bauernfamilie des Christen Nutli im typischen Baustil eines Prättigauer Bauernhauses mit viereckigen Kanthölzern errichtet. Im Laufe der Jahrhunderte verfiel das Anwesen, bis es 1918 Dr. Fritz Schoellhorn aus Winterthur erwarb und liebevoll restaurieren ließ. 1953 schenkte es Dr. Schoellhorn der Gemeinde. Seitdem ist das Nutli Hüschi als Heimatmuseum öffentlich zugänglich und ein hervorragendes Beispiel des bäuerlichen Lebensraums. Im Erdgeschoß liegt hinter der quadratischen Stube mit kleinen Fenstern die Küche. Im Obergeschoß gibt es eine Schlafkammer und eine Webstube.

Ce chalet, situé sur le chemin du restaurant «Alpenrösli» à Klosters, est l'un des plus anciens des Grisons. La bâtisse construite en 1565 par une famille de paysans du coin, les Nutli, dans le style typique de la vallée du Prättigau – la charpente en bois équarri à poutres quadrangulaires est toujours apparente –, avait fini par se délabrer faute d'entretien. Mais en 1918 Fritz Schoellhorn de Winterthur en fit l'acquisition et la restaura avec beaucoup de soin. En 1953, il en fit don à la commune. Depuis, ce magnifique exemple d'habitat montagnard a été ouvert au public. Au rez-de-chaussée, la cuisine est attenante au petit salon éclairé par des fenêtres carrées; à l'étage, se trouvent une chambre et une petite pièce réservée au tissage.

Links: Die bleigefaßten Butzenscheiben sind kleine Glasscheiben mit einer Verdickung in der Mitte, dem »Butzen«.

Left: "Butzenscheiben" or bull's eye windows are small panes of glass with a bulge (or "Butzen") in the middle, held in place by strips of lead.

A gauche: Les vitres en culs de bouteilles bordées de plomb sont des carreaux en verre, comportant un épaississement au centre (le «Butzen»).

Rechts: Im Eingangsbereich des Vorhauses hängen Schlitten, Speisebeutel, Pferdegeschirr und ein »Trinkette« genanntes Holzfäßchen.

Right: Around the entrance to the house hang sledges, food bags, harnesses and a little wooden drinking vessel known as a "Trinkette".

A droite: A l'entrée de la maison sont suspendus une luge, une sacs à nourriture, un harnais et un récipient en bois sont appelé «Trinkette».

Rechts: Auf der fein geschnitzten Stabelle ruht ein Holzkasten von 1657 mit getrockneten Kräutern.

Right: Standing on a finely carved "Stabelle" or chair, herbs have been left to dry in a wooden box dating from 1657.

A droite: Une caisse en bois contenant des herbes séchées et datant de 1657 a été posée sur une «Stabelle», un tabouret finement sculpté.

Unten: Die sogenannte »Kuhschwanzuhr« stammt von 1680. *Rechte Seite:* Die Arventäfelung in der Stube ist 300 Jahre alt.

Below: This so-called "cow's tail" clock dates from 1680. *Facing page:* The Swiss pine panelling in the living room is 300 years old.

Ci-dessous: Cette horloge bien particulière (dite «horloge en queue de vache») date de 1680. *Page de droite:* Les boiseries en pin arolle du salon sont tricentenaires.

Links: Gießfäßchen und Krüge stammen aus der Töpferwerkstatt der Familie Lötscher aus dem nahegelegenen Dorf St. Antönien und sind aus dem 19. Jahrhundert.

Left: The 19th-century urns and jugs come from the Lötscher family pottery in the nearby village St. Antönien.

A gauche: Le petit récipient à bec verseur et les cruches ont été fabriqués au 19e siècle dans l'atelier de céramique de la famille Lötscher du village voisin de St. Antönien.

Folgende Doppelseite: Im Schlafzimmer steht ein altes Arvenhimmelbett.

Following pages: In the bedroom is an antique fourposter bed in Swiss pine.

Double page suivante: La chambre du premier étage, avec son vieux lit à baldaquin en bois de pin arolle.

La Bosca – the "house in the forest" – has been in the Pedrini family since 1890. The present owner, Romano Pedrini of St. Moritz, is a master carpenter specialising in the conversion of old houses. With family and friends, he uses the former "Maiensäss" as a hunting lodge. In the olden days, the cowherd would spend the spring at the "Maiensäss" with his cows. With loving care, Pedrini has made the place more comfortable while respecting the original style. He installed old wooden panelling in the bedroom himself, and only added light switches when he came across some antique originals. The property also includes around ten hectares of land, mostly forest. Neighbouring landowners graze their sheep in the clearings. Here time seems to have stood still.

Romano Pedrini

La Bosca, das Waldhaus, befindet sich schon seit 1890 im Familienbesitz der Pedrini. Der jetzige Hausherr, Romano Pedrini aus St. Moritz, ist ein auf den Ausbau von alten Häusern spezialisierter Schreinermeister. Er nutzt den ehemaligen Maiensäss, in dem früher der Hirte das Frühjahr mit seinen Kühen verbrachte, mit Familie und Freunden als Jagdhütte. Mit viel Liebe hat Pedrini das Gebäude komfortabel gestaltet und dabei doch alles beim alten belassen. Das Schlafzimmer hat er selbst mit altem Holz neu getäfelt. Lichtschalter wurden erst angebracht, als er alte Originale gefunden hatte. Zum Haus gehören ungefähr zehn Hektar Land, die hauptsächlich aus Wald bestehen. In den Lichtungen weiden benachbarte Landwirte ihre Schafe. Hier scheint die Zeit stehengeblieben zu sein.

La Bosca, un chalet situé sur un ancien alpage, appartient à la famille Pedrini depuis 1890. L'actuel maître des lieux, Romano Pedrini, est un ébéniste de Saint-Moritz spécialisé dans la restauration des maisons anciennes. Ce chalet, où logeaient autrefois les vachers au printemps, sert aujourd'hui de pavillon de chasse à la famille Pedrini et à ses amis. Pedrini l'a restauré soigneusement sans toucher toutefois à la substance d'origine. Il a refait lui-même les boiseries de la chambre avec de vieilles pièces de bois et a même installé d'anciens interrupteurs. La maison se trouve sur un terrain boisé de dix hectares, entrecoupé de clairières où paissent des troupeaux de moutons. Ici, le temps donne l'impression de s'être arrêté.

Alpen Interieurs   Romano Pedrini

Vorhergehende Doppelseite: *Das Maiensäss La Bosca, ein Engadiner Hirtenhaus, liegt im Bergell, das den Oberengadin mit Italien verbindet. Der Besitzer Romano Pedrini nutzt es heute als Jagdhütte.*
Linke Seite: *Jagdtrophäen unter dem Giebel; Ruhepause bei der Jagd.*
Oben: *Von der Terrasse hat man einen herrlichen Blick hinab ins Bergell.*

Previous pages: *La Bosca, a former "Maiensäss" or Engadine cowherd's refuge, stands in the Bregaglia Valley, which divides the Upper Engadine from Italy. The owner, Romano Pedrini, uses the house as a hunting lodge.*
Facing page: *hunting trophies under the gable; taking a break during the hunting season.*
Above: *From the terrace there is a glorious view over the Bregaglia Valley.*

Double page précédente: *La Bosca, un ancien «Maiensäss» ou chalet d'alpage, est niché dans la vallée de Bergell qui relie la haute Engadine à l'Italie. Elle sert de pavillon de chasse au propriétaire Romano Pedrini.*
Page de gauche: *trophées exposés sous le pignon; une pause pendant la période de la chasse.*
Ci-dessus: *La terrasse offre une vue à couper le souffle sur la vallée de Bergell.*

Gern lädt der Hausherr, ein begeisterter Koch am Holzofen, Freunde
an den großen Tisch vor dem Haus ein.

Romano Pedrini enjoys cooking on his wood-burning stove and entertaining friends at the huge picnic table in front of the house.

Le maître de maison aime régaler ses amis en cuisinant sur le foyer
chauffé au bois.

Alpen Interieurs   Romano Pedrini

Das Kaminzimmer im Erdgeschoß wird nur bei wirklich schlechtem Wetter benutzt, denn das Leben findet im allgemeinen draußen in der Natur statt.

The cosy living room with an open hearth is only used when the weather is unusually bad. Life at La Bosca is mostly lived outdoors.

La pièce située au niveau inférieur ne sert de refuge qu'en cas d'intempérie puisque la vie se passe en principe dans la nature environnante.

Die Küche von La Bosca. Der Holzofen dient als Kochstelle und als Heizquelle für das gesamte Haus. Der Schüttstein ist mehr als 150 Jahre alt.

The wood-burning stove in the kitchen at La Bosca is used both for cooking and for heating the whole house. The sink is more than 150 years old.

La cuisine de La Bosca. Le poêle à bois permet à la fois de cuisiner et de chauffer la maison. La paillasse de l'évier a plus de 150 ans.

Against the awesome backdrop of the Austrian Ötztal Alps, a cheerful, brightly-coloured house can be seen for miles around. Pizzinini, born in the nearby village, and her partner Luxemburg – both architects – designed the building at their Los Angeles office; they also have branches in Vienna and Luxembourg. They use the place at weekends and to take time off for creative thinking. For their nieces and nephews, who love to come up from the village to visit, the airy house is a paradise. The forms are clearly borrowed from local architecture, the red oriel is a modern interpretation of one at her parents' home, and the dry stone wall is built of layers of Ötztal alpine rock. The house mirrors the colours of the local region. To achieve this, Regina Pizzinini gathered flowers from the mountain meadows of the Tyrol and mixed the paints for the house until they matched exactly with the flowers.

Regina Pizzinini und Leon Luxemburg

Von der gewaltigen Kulisse der Ötztaler Alpen hebt sich verblüffend fröhlich ein buntes Haus ab, das man schon von weitem sieht. Das Architektenpaar Pizzinini-Luxemburg hat sein Haus in Los Angeles entworfen, wo sie wie in Wien und Luxemburg ein Architekturbüro betreiben. Regina Pizzinini, die aus dem Dorf stammt, und Leon Luxemberg nutzen ihr Domizil an Wochenenden und für kreative Pausen. Für die Nichten und Neffen aus dem Dorf, die gern zu Besuch kommen, ist das luftige Haus ein Paradies. Die Gebäudeformen sind eindeutig der lokalen Architektur entlehnt: der rote Erker ist eine moderne Interpretation des Erkers von Regina Pizzininis Elternhaus, die Steinmauer ohne Betonverfugung bilden Felsen der Ötztaler Ache, und auch die Farben stammen aus der örtlichen Natur. Regina Pizzinini hat auf den Tiroler Bergwiesen Blumen gepflückt und die Farben für das Haus so lange mischen lassen, bis sie den Blütentönen genau entsprachen.

De loin déjà, cette maison sertie dans le fabuleux décor du massif de l'Ötztal, dans les Alpes autrichiennes, frappe par ses couleurs et son caractère gai. Les architectes Leon Luxemburg et Regina Pizzinini – native du village où se trouve la maison – l'ont dessinée à Los Angeles où, comme à Vienne et à Luxembourg, le couple possède une agence d'architectes. Ils y passent leurs week-ends ou s'y retirent pour trouver l'inspiration. Pour les neveux et nièces qui habitent dans le village, la maison, par son caractère léger et aéré, est un vrai paradis. Les formes s'inspirent à l'évidence de l'architecture vernaculaire ; le balcon en encorbellement, de couleur rouge, est une interprétation moderne de la maison des parents de Regina. Le mur est construit avec des pierres de la région, sans jointures au béton. Les couleurs, intenses, tirent elles aussi leur origine de la nature environnante. Pour ce faire, Regina Pizzinini est allée cueillir des fleurs dans les pâturages du Tyrol, puis a fait mélanger les couleurs jusqu'à ce qu'elles coïncident parfaitement avec celles des fleurs.

Eingangsseiten: *Treppen, Kuben, klare und kraftvolle Farben bestimmen das innere und äußere Erscheinungsbild des Hauses. Die Räume gehen offen ineinander über.*
Vorhergehende Doppelseite: *Von der Leseecke schweift der Blick weit in die bäuerliche Landschaft und auf die Ötztaler Alpen.*
Linke Seite und oben: *Die blaue Küche bildet den Mittelpunkt des großen Raumes. Das Schlafzimmer ist in diesen Raum »hineingestellt«.*
Rechts: *Auch die Möbel sind Eigenentwürfe.*

First pages: *Staircases, cuboid shapes and strong, bright colours define the interior and exterior mood of the house. The rooms open one into another.*
Previous pages: *view from a reading corner across the broad rural landscape to the Ötztal Alps.*
Facing page and above: *The blue kitchen is the focal point of the generous space, which also incorporates the bedroom.*
Right: *Pizzinini and Luxemburg designed the furniture too.*

Première double page : *Les escaliers, les cubes et les couleurs vigoureuses déterminent la physionomie interne et externe de la maison. Les pièces se présentent comme une suite d'espaces ouverts.*
Double page précédente : *Le coin lecture offre une vaste perspective sur la campagne et le massif de l'Ötztal.*
Page de gauche et ci-dessus : *La cuisine bleue occupe une place centrale dans la grande pièce, où a été également installée la chambre à coucher.*
A droite : *Le mobilier est une création des maîtres de maison.*

Thaddaeus Ropac, dynamic gallery owner and art dealer with interests in Salzburg, Paris and New York, is highly successful and forever on the move. Nevertheless, amid all the hustle and bustle, he always cherished the dream of a certain house – one with which, as a very young man, he had fallen in love at first sight and which for many years lay beyond his reach: Villa Emslieb, a jewel of the baroque era, right next door to Hellbrunn Castle. In August 1996, Ropac, a man who never loses sight of his ultimate goal, held a suitable housewarming for his new home in the form of a light-hearted dinner party for the New York artist Julian Schnabel in the hall of mirrors, where Wolfgang Amadeus Mozart once played for the delectation of the assembled company. Built in 1619 for Archbishop Marcus Sitticus, Emslieb has been recorded in official registers variously as a manor house, "a palace built in the Italian style", a stately home and a castle. For Ropac, Villa Emslieb is the house in which he has been able to realise his vision of an intimate combination of life and art.

Thaddaeus Ropac

Als Galerist und Kunsthändler in Salzburg, Paris und New York tätig, ist Thaddaeus Ropac äußerst erfolgreich und ständig unterwegs. Trotz seines unruhigen Lebens erhielt er sich den Traum von einem Haus, in das er sich als sehr junger Mann auf den ersten Blick verliebt hatte und das lange unerreichbar blieb: Villa Emslieb, ein Kleinod des Barock, in unmittelbarer Nähe des erzbischöflichen Lustschlosses Hellbrunn gelegen. Im August 1996 konnte Ropac – ein Mann, der nie sein Ziel aus den Augen verliert – sein neues Domizil comme il faut einweihen: mit einem amüsanten Diner zu Ehren des New Yorker Künstlers Julian Schnabel im Spiegelsaal, wo einst Wolfgang Amadeus Mozart zur Freude der Gäste aufspielte. Im Jahre 1619 für Erzbischof Marcus Sitticus erbaut, wurde Emslieb in Dokumenten mal als Herrenhaus, mal als »in italienischer Art erbauter Palast«, als Adelssitz oder Schloß bezeichnet. In seiner Villa Emslieb hat Ropac seiner Vision vom Leben mit Kunst sehr nah kommen können.

Le galeriste et marchand d'art Thaddaeus Ropac est un homme alerte et heureux en affaires. Bien qu'il soit toujours par monts et par vaux – il partage son temps entre Salzbourg, Paris et New York –, il a sans cesse gardé l'espoir d'habiter la maison de ses rêves: la Villa Emslieb, un petit joyau du baroque situé à proximité du château de plaisance de Hellbrunn dont il était tombé amoureux dans sa jeunesse et qui resta longtemps inaccessible. En août 1996, Ropac, un homme qui ne perd jamais de vue son objectif, s'installe enfin à Emslieb. Pour célébrer l'événement, il donne un dîner amusant pour l'artiste new-yorkais Julian Schnabel dans la salle des glaces où, en son temps, Wolfgang Amadeus Mozart avait régalé les invités de sa virtuosité. L'histoire d'Emslieb remonte à 1619, année où elle fut construite pour l'archevêque Marcus Sitticus. Les documents de l'époque la décrivent tantôt comme un manoir, tantôt comme «un palais de style italien» ou bien encore comme un château ou une demeure noble. Pour Ropac, la Villa Emslieb est tout simplement la maison qui incarne le mieux sa vision d'une vie en accord avec l'art.

Vorhergehende Doppelseite, links: *Ein Hase von Barry Flanagan posiert in einer Stucknische im Erdgeschoß.*
Vorhergehende Doppelseite, rechts: *Villa Emslieb mit Park; Blick durch den Säulenportikus des Eingangs auf eine Skulptur von Anne und Patrick Poirier.*
Oben: *Blick auf den Park mit Skulpturen von Robert Wilson, Mimmo Paladino, Antony Gormley, Anne und Patrick Poirier.*
Rechts: *das Treppenhaus; ein weiteres Werk von Barry Flanagan im Vorraum im ersten Geschoß.*
Rechte Seite: *Blick in den frühlingshaften Park.*

Previous pages, left: *A hare sculpted by Barry Flanagan stands proudly in a stuccoed niche on the ground floor.*
Previous pages, right: *Villa Emslieb and its surrounding park; a sculpture by Anne and Patrick Poirier glimpsed through the colonnaded porch at the front of the house.*
Above: *view across the park with sculptures by Robert Wilson, Mimmo Paladino, Antony Gormley, Anne and Patrick Poirier.*
Right: *the staircase; a work by Barry Flanagan on the first-floor landing.*
Facing page: *view of the park in spring.*

Double page précédente, à gauche: *Un lièvre de Barry Flanagan se dresse fièrement dans une niche en stuc du rez-de-chaussée.*
Double page précédente, à droite: *la Villa Emslieb, avec son parc; une sculpture d'Anne et Patrick Poirier.*
Ci-dessus: *vue sur le parc et les sculptures de Robert Wilson, Mimmo Paladino, Antony Gormley, Anne et Patrick Poirier.*
Ci-dessous: *l'escalier; une œuvre de Barry Flanagan dans le vestibule du premier étage.*
Page de droite: *vue sur le parc au printemps.*

Oben: *Schattenspiel im Treppenhaus. Vier kleinformatige Arbeiten von Imi Knoebel.*
Rechts: *Blick in die Gewölbe der Eingangshalle mit Kunstwerken von Alex Katz, Andy Warhol, Imi Knoebel und Joseph Beuys.*
Rechte Seite: *Neben und über dem Marmorkamin in der Eingangshalle befinden sich Werke von Imi Knoebel und Andy Warhol.*

Above: *shadow play on the staircase. Four small works by Imi Knoebel.*
Right: *view of the vaulted entrance hall with works by Alex Katz, Andy Warhol, Imi Knoebel and Joseph Beuys.*
Facing page: *alongside the marble fireplace in the entrance hall, works by Imi Knoebel and Andy Warhol.*

Ci-dessus: *jeux d'ombres dans l'escalier. Au mur, quatre petites œuvres d'Imi Knoebel.*
A droite: *le hall d'entrée voûté, avec des œuvres d'Alex Katz, Andy Warhol, Imi Knoebel et Joseph Beuys.*
Page de droite: *au-dessus et à côté de la cheminée du hall, des œuvres d'Imi Knoebel et d'Andy Warhol.*

Linke Seite: das Arbeitszimmer von Thaddaeus Ropac mit Vasen-
objekten von Mimmo Paladino, »Flowers« von Andy Warhol und
zwei Bildern von Julius Deutschbauer. Unter dem Fenster steht eine
Bank von Josef Hoffmann mit einem Bezug von Rona Pondick.
Oben: das Eßzimmer mit einem Aubusson-Teppich und Thonet-
Stühlen. Auf dem Tisch eine Skulptur von Michèle Blondel, rechts
neben dem Fenster ein Bild von Sandro Chia und rechts ein Werk von
Imi Knoebel.
Rechts: Blick in das Arbeitszimmer.

Facing page: Thaddaeus Ropac's study, with vases by Mimmo
Paladino and "Flowers" by Andy Warhol. Under the window is a
bench designed by Josef Hoffmann with a cover by Rona Pondick.
To the left of the window are two paintings by Julius Deutschbauer.
Above: the dining room with an Aubusson carpet and Thonet chairs.
On the table is a sculpture by Michèle Blondel, near the window a
painting by Sandro Chia, and on the right a work by Imi Knoebel.
Right: looking into the study.

Page de gauche: le bureau de Thaddaeus Ropac. Les vases sont de
Mimmo Paladino, le tableau «Flowers» est d'Andy Warhol. Sous la
fenêtre, un banc de Josef Hoffmann avec une garniture de Rona
Pondick. A gauche de la fenêtre, deux tableaux de Julius Deutschbauer.
Ci-dessus: la salle à manger avec une tapisserie d'Aubusson et des
sièges Thonet. Sur la table, une sculpture de Michèle Blondel; près de
la fenêtre, sur la droite, un tableau de Sandro Chia et à droite, une
œuvre d'Imi Knoebel.
A droite: vue sur le bureau de Thaddaeus Ropac.

Oben: *Sitzgruppe im kleinen Salon.*
Rechte Seite: *Im großen Spiegelsaal im zweiten Geschoß spielte schon Wolfgang Amadeus Mozart. Heute gibt hier Thaddaeus Ropac zu Ehren seiner internationalen Künstler und Klientel seine berühmten, ebenso amüsanten wie interessanten Diners für bis zu sechzig Personen.*

Above: *table and chairs in the small drawing room.*
Facing page: *Wolfgang Amadeus Mozart once played in the great hall of mirrors on the second floor. Today the room provides the setting for Thaddaeus Ropac's famous and highly entertaining dinner parties for up to sixty guests, given in honour of celebrities from his international circle of artists and clients.*

Ci-dessus: *le petit salon, avec table et fauteuils.*
Page de droite: *la grande salle des glaces où Wolfgang Amadeus Mozart donna des concerts. Aujourd'hui, Thaddaeus Ropac y invite à ses fameux dîners jusqu'à soixante personnes choisies parmi sa clientèle d'acheteurs et d'artistes.*

Oben links: *Blick in die Gästetoilette im ersten Geschoß mit kleiner Bibliothek und schwarzem Marmorboden.*
Oben rechts: *Im Schlafzimmer verbirgt sich hinter der Schrankwand und dem Wandabschluß aus mattem Glas ein komfortables Bad.*
Rechte Seite: *Die Küche mit Originaleinbauten hat Ropac fast unsichtbar mit raffinierter Technik ergänzen lassen.*

Above left: *the guest cloakroom on the first floor with a small library and black marble floor.*
Above right: *The built-in wardrobes and opaque glass in the bedroom conceal a luxurious bathroom.*
Facing page: *In the kitchen with its original built-in units, Ropac has installed sophisticated technology which remains almost invisible.*

Ci-dessus, à gauche: *les toilettes du premier étage, avec une petite bibliothèque et un sol en marbre noir.*
Ci-dessus, à droite: *la chambre, avec une salle de bains confortable dissimulée derrière des éléments muraux en verre dépoli.*
Page de droite: *la cuisine et ses meubles encastrés d'origine, que Ropac a modernisée et complétée de façon quasi invisible grâce à une technique raffinée.*

For decades, the ancestral home of the Sertoli Salis family, built in about 1665 at Tirano in Italy's Valtellina region, not far from St. Moritz, was used only as a summer residence. In the nick of time, when the great baroque manor house was on the point of collapse, Conte Cesare Sertoli Salis and his brother Francesco decided to act to save the family's treasured possession. Today, the Palazzo Salis is not only their home once again, but they have also revived the old family business of viticulture and wine trading. Room by room, the house is being painstakingly restored. Some of the drawing rooms and the chapel are already open to the public. Particularly romantic is a flower garden in the old Italian style, laid out around a fountain. The old frescoes are especially attractive; their numerous trompe l'œil perspectives, false windows and doors continually confuse visitors as they wander from one room to the next.

Conte Cesare Sertoli Salis

Jahrzehntelang nutzte die Familie Sertoli Salis ihr um 1665 erbautes Stammhaus in Tirano, im italienischen Veltlin unweit von St. Moritz gelegen, nur noch als Sommerresidenz. Gerade rechtzeitig vor dem endgültigen Verfall des großen barocken Herrenhauses besannen sich Conte Cesare Sertoli Salis und sein Bruder Francesco auf die Preziose im Familienbesitz. Heute ist der Palazzo Salis nicht nur wieder ihr Zuhause, sie haben auch das alte Familiengeschäft erfolgreich wiederbelebt, den Weinbau und -handel. Raum für Raum wird sorgfältig restauriert. Schon heute sind einige Säle und die Kapelle auch der Öffentlichkeit zugänglich. Besonders romantisch ist der um einen Brunnen angelegte alte italienische Blumengarten. Die reizvollen originalen Fresken mit ihren zahlreichen Scheinarchitekturen, falschen Fenstern und Türen führen den Besucher immer wieder aufs neue hinters Licht.

Pendant longtemps, la demeure familiale des Sertoli Salis, construite en 1665 à Tirano, dans la province italienne de Valteline, non loin de Saint-Moritz, ne servit que de résidence d'été. C'est encore à temps, avant que cette demeure de style baroque ne tombe en ruine, que le comte Cesare Sertoli Salis et son frère Francesco prirent conscience de sa valeur. Ils en ont fait à nouveau leur résidence principale et ont relancé l'affaire familiale: la production et le commerce du vin. La restauration, pièce par pièce, du «palazzo» se poursuit avec un soin tout particulier; quelques salons ainsi que la chapelle sont d'ores et déjà ouverts au public. Le jardin à l'italienne agrémenté d'une fontaine respire le romantisme, et les anciennes fresques qui leurrent toujours le visiteur avec leurs perspectives en trompe-l'œil, leurs fausses portes et leurs fausses fenêtres, ont beaucoup de charme.

Vorhergehende Doppelseite, links: *Conte Cesare Sertoli Salis; die Gartenfassade des im 17. Jahrhundert erbauten Palazzo Salis.*
Vorhergehende Doppelseite, rechts: *Die Wendeltreppe an der Wand des großen Ehrensaals ist gemalt.*
Oben: *Über dem barocken Kamin im »saloncello«, dem Kleinen Salon, prangen die Wappen der Familienallianz Salis-Zizers und Wolkenstein aus dem Jahre 1695. Die Portieren sind Illusionsmalerei.*
Rechte Seite: *Die Fresken des »saloncello« entstanden im 17. Jahrhundert.*

Previous pages, left: *Conte Cesare Sertoli Salis; the 17th-century palazzo's garden side.*
Previous pages, right: *The spiral staircase on the wall of the great formal salon is a trompe l'œil.*
Above: *The resplendent coat of arms symbolising the alliance of the Salis-Zizers and Wolkenstein families in 1695 stands above the baroque fireplace in the "saloncello" or Small Salon. The doors on the left of the fireplace are trompe l'œil.*
Facing page: *The frescoes in the "saloncello" were painted in the 17th century.*

Double page précédente, à gauche: *le comte Cesare Sertoli Salis; côté jardin, la façade du Palazzo Salis, construit au 17e siècle.*
Double page précédente, à droite: *L'escalier en colimaçon du grand salon d'honneur est un décor en trompe-l'œil.*
Ci-dessus: *La cheminée baroque du «saloncello», le Petit salon, est surmontée des armoiries des familles Salis-Zizers et Wolkenstein qui firent alliance en 1695. Les portières sont peintes en trompe-l'œil.*
Page de droite: *Les fresques du «saloncello» datent du 17e siècle.*

Vorhergehende Doppelseite: *die Ehrenhalle mit prachtvollen Fresken von Carlo Innocenzo Carlone (ca. 1686–1775). Die Möbel stammen aus dem 17. und 18. Jahrhundert. Gelegentlich finden hier öffentliche Konzerte und Konferenzen statt.*
Oben: *Der private Teil des Palazzo wird von drei Familienzweigen genutzt, von zwei Brüdern und einem Cousin, und ist – unsichtbar – mit allem modernen Komfort ausgestattet. Die Salons sind mit Möbeln aus dem 16. bis 18. Jahrhundert eingerichtet.*
Rechts: *Der Treppenaufgang im zentralen Teil des Palazzo aus dem 17. Jahrhundert ist von illusionistischen Fresken gekrönt, die eine große Kuppel darstellen.*

Previous pages: *The formal hall contains superb frescoes by Carlo Innocenzo Carlone (c. 1686–1775). The furniture dates from the 17th and 18th centuries. Public concerts and conferences are occasionally held here.*
Above: *The Palazzo's private apartments are occupied by three branches of the family, two brothers and a cousin, and are equipped with all mod cons – albeit very discreetly. The drawing room furniture dates from between the 16th and 18th centuries.*
Right: *Above the Palazzo's central staircase are 17th-century frescoes, creating the illusion of a large dome.*

Double page précédente: *le hall d'honneur, avec de splendides fresques de Carlo Innocenzo Carlone (c. 1686–1775). De temps à autre, on y donne des conférences et des concerts publics.*
Ci-dessus: *La partie privée du Palazzo Salis où logent trois branches de la famille, deux frères et un cousin, est d'un confort moderne mais discret. L'ameublement des salons date des 16e, 17e et 18e siècles.*
A droite: *Le grand escalier du « palazzo », qui date du 17e siècle, est couronné de fresques donnant l'illusion d'une coupole.*

Rechts: die Weinkeller des familieneigenen Weinguts Conti Sertoli Salis.
Unten: In der Probierstube können die Erzeugnisse des Weinguts verkostet werden. Die Rot- und Weißweine werden nach alten Methoden und unter ökologischen Gesichtspunkten angebaut und gehören zu den besten der Region.

Right: the cellars of the Conti Sertoli Salis' family wine-growing estate.
Below: The products can be sampled in the tasting room. The red and white wines, ecologically produced by time-honoured methods, are among the best in the region.

A droite: vue des chais du domaine Conti Sertoli Salis.
Ci-dessous: La dégustation des vins se fait dans cette salle. Les vins, rouges et blancs, sont produits selon des méthodes anciennes et des préoccupations écologiques. Ils comptent parmi les meilleurs de la région.

The painter Giovanni Segantini was born in Trentino in 1858 and died in the Engadine in 1899. It was only in 1895, a few years before his death, that the artist, ever in search of ideal light, came to Maloja with his family. He bought the chalet, built in Italianate Art Deco style by the Bernese architect Kuoni for Count Renesse, and added his own semicircular studio extension. Here he produced the sketches for his best-known work, the Triptych "Nature, Life, Death", now housed in the Segantini Museum in St. Moritz. The artist's wife, Bice, was a member of the Bugatti family. Her brother Carlo was the pioneering furniture designer, and his son Ettore was creator of the famous cars. Segantini's studio is now a museum. The large chalet, built of larch on a rock foundation, is now occupied by the painter's descendants, among them his great-granddaughter Ragnhild Segantini, an international art and wine consultant.

Ragnhild Segantini

Der Maler Giovanni Segantini, 1858 im Trentin geboren und 1899 im Engadin gestorben, kam auf der ewigen Suche nach dem Licht erst 1895, also wenige Jahre vor seinem Tod, mit seiner Familie nach Maloja. Er erwarb das von dem Berner Architekten Kuoni im Stil der Art déco à l'italienne für den Grafen Renesse erbaute Chalet und ergänzte es mit einem halbrunden Atelier. Hier entstanden die Skizzen für sein bekanntestes Werk, das Triptychon »Natur, Leben, Tod«, das heute im Segantini-Museum von St. Moritz zu sehen ist. Bice, die Frau des Künstlers, war eine geborene Bugatti, ihr Bruder Carlo der bahnbrechende Möbeldesigner, dessen Sohn Ettore der berühmte Autokonstrukteur. Heute ist Segantinis Atelier Museum. Das große Chalet aus Lärchenholz auf Felssockel wird von den Nachkommen des Malers bewohnt, insbesondere von der Urenkelin Ragnhild Segantini, die als internationale Kunst- und Wein-Konsultantin arbeitet.

Perpétuellement en quête de lumière, le peintre Giovanni Segantini (né en 1858 dans le Trentin et décédé en 1899 en Engadine) se retira sur le Maloja avec sa famille en 1895, peu de temps avant sa mort. Il fit l'acquisition d'un chalet construit dans le style Art déco italien par l'architecte bernois Kuoni pour le comte Renesse et lui ajouta un atelier demi-circulaire. C'est dans cet atelier que les esquisses de son œuvre la plus connue virent le jour. Le «Triptyque des Alpes (la nature, la vie, la mort)» est aujourd'hui exposé au musée Segantini de Saint-Moritz. Bice, la femme du peintre, était une Bugatti, son frère Carlo, le fameux créateur de meubles, et le fils de celui-ci, Ettore, le célèbre constructeur automobile. L'atelier de Segantini est devenu un musée. Les descendants de l'artiste, et particulièrement son arrière-petite-fille Ragnhild Segantini, consultante internationale en art et en vins, habitent ce grand chalet en mélèze reposant sur un soubassement en roche.

Eingangsseiten: Chalet und Atelier von Giovanni Segantini.
Vorhergehende Doppelseite, links: *Im Atelier steht auf Segantinis Staffelei ein Porträt seines ältesten Sohnes Gottardo; Blick auf den Atelier-Rundbau von Giovanni Segantini vor dem Chalet.*
Vorhergehende Doppelseite, rechts: *Das Relief in der »Piano-Veranda« schuf Mario Segantini, der zweite Sohn Giovannis. Es zeigt Mario Segantinis Frau Marina.*
Oben: *Der »salotto«, der Salon, ist der Lieblingsraum der heutigen Besitzerin Ragnhild Segantini. Das mit grünem Samt bezogene Sofa schuf der berühmte Möbeldesigner Carlo Bugatti, der Schwager Segantinis.*

First pages: *Giovanni Segantini's rotunda studio and the chalet.*
Previous pages, left: *A portrait of Segantini's eldest son Gottardo is displayed on an easel in the studio; the studio and the chalet.*

Previous pages, right: *The relief in the "Piano-Veranda" is by Mario Segantini, Giovanni's second son, and portrays his wife, Marina.*
Above: *The "salotto", or drawing room is present owner Ragnhild Segantini's favourite room. The sofa covered with green velvet is by the famous furniture designer Carlo Bugatti, Segantini's brother-in-law.*

Première double page: *l'atelier et le chalet de Giovanni Segantini.*
Double page précédente, à gauche: *portrait du fils aîné du peintre, Gottardo, posé sur un chevalet; l'atelier et le chalet.*
Double page précédente, à droite: *Le relief, dans la « véranda au piano» est une œuvre de Mario Segantini, le second fils de Giovanni; il représente sa femme Marina.*
Ci-dessus: *Le « salotto», le salon, est la pièce préférée de l'actuelle propriétaire Ragnhild Segantini. Le canapé en velours vert est du célèbre créateur de meubles Carlo Bugatti, beau-frère de Segantini.*

Eßtisch im »Salotto«. Stühle und Tisch entwarf Carlo Bugatti gemeinsam mit Giovanni Segantini. Die italienische Anrichte stammt aus einer Sakristei. Darauf befinden sich Familiensilber, Porzellan und japanische Vasen. Die Deckenleuchte mit Engeln aus Bronze ist von dem Bildhauer Rembrandt Bugatti, Carlos Bruder. Auf dem Tisch stehen Murano-Gläser mit den Familieninitialen.

The dining table and chairs in the "salotto" were designed by Carlo Bugatti and Giovanni Segantini, the Italian sideboard came from a sacristy. On it are the family silver, pieces of porcelain and Japanese vases. The bronze angel hanging lamp is by the sculptor Rembrandt Bugatti, Carlo's brother, and the Murano glasses on the table bear the family initials.

La table du «salotto». Les chaises et la table sont une création commune de Carlo Bugatti et de Giovanni Segantini. Le bahut est un meuble de sacristie italien sur lequel sont placés de l'argenterie familiale, de la porcelaine et des vases japonais. La suspension décorée d'anges en bronze est du sculpteur Rembrandt Bugatti, le frère de Carlo. Sur la table, des verres de Murano portent les initiales de la famille.

Links: *Giovanni Segantinis Mal-utensilien inklusive seines Ruck-sacks. Er malte stets in der freien Natur.*

Left: *Giovanni Segantini's painting utensils and his ruck-sack. He always painted in the open air.*

A gauche: *le matériel de pein-ture de Giovanni Segantini et son sac à dos. L'artiste peignait toujours en pleine nature.*

Rechts: *eine italienische Kom-mode mit alten Kupfergeräten. An der Wand hängen Jagd-trophäen und alte Skier.*

Right: *Italian chest with old copper pieces. On the wall, hunting trophies and old skis.*

A droite: *une commode italienne, avec de vieux cuivres. Sur le mur, des trophées de chasse et de vieux skis.*

Rechts: *Das Porträt von Baronin Mathilde Krug von Nidda, Gottardo Segantinis Frau, hängt in der Veranda.*

Right: *A portrait of Gottardo Segantini's wife, Baroness Mathilde Krug von Nidda, hangs on one of the verandas.*

A droite: *dans une véranda, un portrait de la femme de Gottardo Segantini, la baronne Mathilde Krug von Nidda.*

Links: *Im »salotto« stehen Mö-bel von Carlo Bugatti und Gio-vanni Segantini. Die Lampe mit Bronzeengeln stammt von Rembrandt Bugatti.*

Left: *in the "salotto"; furniture by Carlo Bugatti and Giovanni Segantini, and a lamp with bronze angels by Rembrandt Bugatti.*

A gauche: *Les meubles du « sa-lotto » sont de Carlo Bugatti et de Giovanni Segantini; la sus-pension aux anges de bronze, de Rembrandt Bugatti.*

Rechts: *im Salon: ein holländi-sches Ölgemälde, Zeichnungen von Segantini und Silberlöffel aus St. Petersburg.*

Right: *in the drawing room: a Dutch oil painting, Segantini drawings and a silver spoon from St. Petersburg.*

A droite: *dans le salon, un tableau à l'huile hollandais, des dessins de Segantini et des cuil-lères en argent de Saint-Pétersbourg.*

Rechts: *Blick in den Garten. Auf dem Fensterbrett silberne Enten aus Sardinien sowie Familiensilber.*

Right: *looking into the garden. On the window sill, silver ducks from Sardinia and family silver.*

A droite: *vue sur le jardin. De-vant la fenêtre, sont posés des canards en argent de Sardaigne et de l'argenterie de famille.*

Links: ein Album mit alten Fotos von Giovanni Segantini. Rechts hängen alte Schneeschuhe.

Left: an album of old photographs of Giovanni Segantini. Hanging on the right, an old pair of snow shoes.

A gauche: un album de photos de Giovanni Segantini; à droite, d'anciennes raquettes de montagnard.

Links: eine Segantini-Büste des Prinzen Trou, dahinter Zeichnungen und ein unvollendetes Gemälde.

Left: a bust of Prince Trou by Segantini; behind it, drawings and an unfinished painting.

A gauche: un buste de Segantini représentant le prince Trou; à l'arrière-plan, des dessins et un tableau inachevé.

Rechts: in der »Piano-Veranda« ein Porträt von Gottardos Töchtern Romana, Graziella und Bice.

Right: on the "piano veranda", a portrait of Gottardo's daughters, Romana, Graziella and Bice.

A droite: Dans la « véranda au piano », se trouvent un portrait des filles de Gottardo – Romana, Graziella et Bice.

Links: Den Stuhl aus Holz, Leder und Metall schufen ebenfalls Carlo Bugatti und Giovanni Segantini.

Left: The wood, leather and metal chair was also designed by Carlo Bugatti and Giovanni Segantini.

A gauche: La chaise en bois, en cuir et en métal est une autre création de Carlo Bugatti et de Giovanni Segantini.

Links: Blick in den Salon mit Möbeln von Bugatti und italienischen Gemälden aus dem 17. Jahrhundert.

Left: view of the drawing room with Bugatti furniture and 17th-century Italian paintings.

A gauche: vue du salon, avec des meubles de Bugatti et des tableaux italiens du 17e siècle.

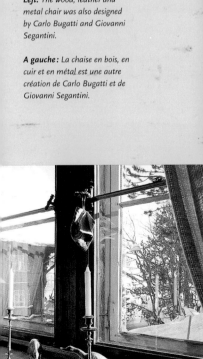

Rechts: das »Renaissance«-Schlafzimmer von Giovanni Segantini und seiner geliebten Frau Bice, geborene Bugatti.

Right: the Renaissance-style bedroom of Giovanni Segantini and his beloved wife Bice, née Bugatti.

A droite: la chambre « Renaissance » du peintre et de sa femme Bice Bugatti

La Ferme d'Hauteluce is a little jewel in the Savoy Alps, not far from the winter sports resort of Megève. Five years ago, Jocelyne and Jean-Louis Sibuet, second-generation hoteliers, refurbished the old farm house and transformed it into a holiday home to let. This cosy and very comfortable refuge boasts a drawing room with open fire, kitchen, dining room, four bedrooms, four bathrooms, swimming pool, sauna, jacuzzi and an office with telephone and fax. Guests also have the option of five-star service with a cook and a daily newspaper. The owner had much of the furniture constructed to his own design using antique materials, while his wife scoured local antique shops and flea markets for the most appealing accessories. The result is a dream home in the mountains, available for rent.

Jocelyne und Jean-Louis Sibuet

La Ferme d'Hauteluce ist ein Kleinod in den Savoyer Alpen, in der Nähe des Wintersportortes Megève. Jocelyne und Jean-Louis Sibuet, Hoteliers in der zweiten Generation, haben den alten Bauernhof vor fünf Jahren als Gästehaus wieder neu aufgebaut. Das sehr komfortable und urgemütliche Refugium umfaßt einen Salon mit offenem Kamin, Küche, Speisezimmer, vier Schlafzimmer, vier Bäder, Pool, Sauna, Jacuzzi und Büro mit Telefon und Fax. Wenn man möchte, wird ein perfekter Service inklusive Koch und Tageszeitung zur Verfügung gestellt. Der Hausherr hat viele Einrichtungsgegenstände selbst entworfen und aus alten Materialien anfertigen lassen. Die Hausherrin hat aus den Antiquitätenläden und Flohmärkten der Gegend die schönsten Wohnaccessoires zusammengetragen. Das Ergebnis ist ein Traum in den Bergen, den man mieten kann.

La Ferme d'Hauteluce est un petit bijou niché dans la montagne, près de Megève, en Haute-Savoie. Jocelyne et Jean-Louis Sibuet, hôteliers de la deuxième génération, ont transformé il y a cinq ans cette vieille ferme en pension. Confortable et agréable, elle comprend un salon avec une cheminée ouverte, une cuisine, une salle à manger, quatre chambres, quatre salles de bains, une piscine, un sauna, des jacuzzis, un bureau avec téléphone et télécopieur. Si le client le désire, il peut même disposer d'un service complet, cuisinier et journal inclus. Une bonne partie du mobilier a été fabriquée à partir de vieux matériaux et d'après les propres plans du propriétaire. Sa femme, de son côté, a couru les antiquaires et les brocantes pour trouver les plus beaux objets de décoration. Le résultat est un chalet de rêve où l'on peut louer des chambres.

Alpen Interieurs   Jocelyne und Jean-Louis Sibuet

Eingangsseiten, links: der Frühstückstisch mit Porzellan und Keramik; alte Keramik aus Savoyen.
Eingangsseiten, rechts: Die Ferme d'Hauteluce schmiegt sich an den Berg und hat einen phantastischen Blick auf die Savoyer Hochalpen.
Vorhergehende Doppelseite: Blick aus der Küche in den Eßbereich und den Salon. Die alten Bauernmöbel ergänzen vom Hausherrn entworfene Stühle. Die Sitzkissen sind mit Flanell bezogen.
Linke Seite: Anrichte mit altem und neuem Keramikgeschirr sowie selbstgemachten Marmeladen.
Oben und rechts: Die Küche ist mit einem modernisierten alten Holzofen ausgestattet. Viele Accessoires stammen von den Flohmärkten der Gegend.

First pages, left: place settings for breakfast with porcelain and ceramic tableware; old ceramics from Savoy.
First pages, right: La Ferme d'Hauteluce nestles in the mountains with a fantastic view of the Savoy Alps.
Previous pages: the dining area and drawing room seen from the kitchen. Rustic antique furniture is complemented by chairs designed by Jean-Louis Sibuet. The benches are covered with flannel.
Facing page: dresser with ancient and modern ceramic tableware and home-made preserves.
Above and right: The kitchen is equipped with an old, but modernised, wood-burning stove. Many of the accessories come from local flea markets.

Première double page, à gauche: un petit-déjeuner servi dans de la vaisselle en porcelaine et en céramique; de la vieille céramique de Savoie.
Première double page, à droite: La ferme est adossée à la montagne, avec une vue magnifique sur les Alpes.

Double page précédente: le coin salle à manger et le salon vus de la cuisine. De vieux meubles rustiques côtoient des chaises créées par le maître de maison. Les bancs sont garnis de flanelle.
Page de gauche: un bahut avec de la céramique ancienne et moderne, et des pots de confiture.
Ci-dessus et ci-dessous: La cuisine est équipée d'un vieux poêle à bois modernisé. De nombreux objets proviennent des marchés aux puces de la région.

Links: *eine eiserne Obst-Etagère.*

Left: *iron fruit rack.*

A gauche: *un présentoir à fruits en fer.*

Rechts: *ein altes Backgammon-Spiel.*

Right: *antique backgammon set.*

A droite: *un vieux jeu de backgammon.*

Rechts: *ein Wandschränkchen mit hölzernen Untersetzern und einigen alten Büchlein.*

Right: *small wall cabinet with wooden coasters and some old books.*

A droite: *une petite armoire murale avec des dessous-de-plat et des dessous-de-verre en bois, et quelques livres anciens.*

Links: *Stilleben in der Küche.*

Left: *still life in the kitchen.*

A gauche: *nature morte dans la cuisine.*

Links: eine alte Anrichte in der Küche.

Left: antique dresser in the kitchen.

A gauche: le vieux bahut de la cuisine.

Links: winterliches Stilleben auf dem Kaminsims.

Left: wintry still-life on the mantlepiece.

A gauche: nature morte hivernale posée sur la tablette de la cheminée.

Rechts: ein niedriger rustikaler Tisch mit einer Kristallkaraffe.

Right: rustic occasional table with crystal carafe.

A droite: une table basse rustique, avec une carafe en cristal.

Links: Das Alkovenbett ist ausgestattet mit karierten amerikanischen Stoffen.

Left: box-bed with American gingham bed linen.

A gauche: l'alcôve, avec la literie en tissu américain à carreaux.

Links: Diesen Kamin hat Jean-Louis Sibuet entworfen.

Left: fireplace designed by Jean-Louis Sibuet.

A gauche: la cheminée créée par Jean-Louis Sibuet.

In 1981, the Munich-based architect and designer Peter Straßl discovered the dilapidated soap-boiler's house in the heart of the village of St. Georgen in the Salzkammergut, barely four kilometres from the Attersee. With the eye of an expert, he recognised that the walls and vaults of the house, built in 1588, most likely for a local craftsman and his family, were still sound. Thanks to careful restoration, Straßl was able to retain the basic structure of the house. Ten rooms are distributed over two floors and there is also a large inner courtyard measuring around 200 square metres, where the Straßls and their guests spend much of their time in summer. The restoration has succeeded in retaining and emphasizing the house's own special character; it has neither been turned into a historic pastiche nor a contemporary design. Peter Straßl and his wife Rixa von Treuenfels, who both lead busy lives in Munich, use the house at weekends and holidays. They love to entertain friends, cook for them, and listen to or play music there – the cross-vaulting provides wonderful acoustics.

Peter Straßl

Peter Straßl, Münchner Architekt und Designer, fand das alte baufällige Seifensiederhaus im Salzkammergut schon 1981. Es liegt im Dorfkern von St. Georgen, keine vier Kilometer vom Attersee entfernt. Mit Kennerblick erkannte Straßl, daß Grundmauern und Gewölbe des 1588 vermutlich für eine einheimische Handwerkerfamilie erbauten Hauses in Ordnung waren. Sorgfältig restauriert konnte die ursprüngliche Struktur unverändert erhalten bleiben. Zehn Räume verteilen sich auf zwei Stockwerke. Außerdem gibt es einen ungefähr 200 Quadratmeter großen Innenhof, in dem sich das Leben im Sommer abspielt. Der eigenwillige Stil des Hauses ist weder historisch ergänzt, noch durch modernes Design verfälscht, sondern geschickt betont worden. Peter Straßl und seine Frau Rixa von Treuenfels, beide in München sehr beschäftigt, nutzen das Haus an den Wochenenden und in den Ferien. Sie laden sich hierher gerne Gäste ein. Dann wird gekocht und musiziert – die Kreuzgratgewölbe haben eine wunderbare Akustik.

L'architecte et designer munichois Peter Straßl découvre dès 1981, dans le Salzkammergut, une ancienne maison de savonnier située au cœur du village de St. Georgen, à moins de quatre kilomètres d'Attersee. Il remarque en connaisseur que cette bâtisse de 1588, sans doute construite à l'origine pour une famille d'artisans, cache sous son apparent délabrement un gros œuvre sain et solide. Les dix pièces de la maison, dont la maçonnerie, les voûtes et la structure ont été soigneusement assainies et restaurées, sont distribuées sur deux niveaux, tout autour d'une cour intérieure de 200 mètres carrés environ, où se déroule la vie en été. Son style très particulier n'a subi aucun ajout historique ni été dénaturé par quelque design moderne: il est juste habilement mis en valeur. Peter Straßl et sa femme, Rixa von Treuenfels, vivent à Munich; leur emploi du temps très chargé ne leur permet de passer que les week-ends et les vacances dans cette maison. C'est pour eux l'occasion de cuisiner, d'écouter de la musique ou même d'en faire: l'acoustique est excellente sous les voûtes d'arête.

Vorhergehende Doppelseite, links: Blick auf das mit Rosen und Geißblatt bewachsene Haus mit dem alten Dorfbrunnen im Vordergrund; eine ruhige Ecke im Garten.
Vorhergehende Doppelseite, rechts: Der von Harry Bertoia entworfene Sessel »Diamond No. 421LU« steht im großen Gästezimmer. Auf der Fensterbank aus Zinkblech Keramiken aus den dreißiger Jahren.
Unten: die Küche mit dem alten Kachelherd. Der Ziegelboden ist gewachst. Auf den umlackierten Bürocontainern liegt ein Hackblock aus Ahornholz, von einer Eisenklammer zusammengehalten.

Previous pages, left: the rose- and honeysuckle-clad house with the old village well; a corner of the garden.
Previous pages, right: This Harry Bertoia armchair "Diamond No. 421LU" is in the large guest room. Thirties' ceramics adorn the sheet-zinc-covered window sill.
Below: The brick-tiled kitchen floor has been waxed, the tiled oven is an old model. An iron-framed maple wood chopping block stands on a repainted filing cabinet.

Première double page, à gauche: la maison, avec ses rosiers et son chèvrefeuille grimpants, et, au premier plan, l'ancienne fontaine du village; un coin du jardin.
Première double page, à droite: le siège «Diamond No. 421LU» de Harry Bertoia dans la grande chambre d'amis. Sur le rebord en zinc laminé de la fenêtre, des céramiques datant des années trente.
Ci-dessous: la cuisine, avec son sol en tomettes cirées; la cuisinière carrelée est très ancienne et les conteneurs de bureau, revernis et convertis en meuble de rangement, sont recouverts d'un bloc d'érable retenu par de longues griffes de fer.

Oben: *der Wohnraum im Erdgeschoß. Um den großen Tisch stehen verschiedene alte Bürostühle. Auf dem Tisch liegt ein Stoff aus Sumatra im traditionellen Ikat-Stil. Unter dem Fenster steht der berühmte »Einschwinger No. B5« von Stefan Wewerka.*
Rechts: *Blick von der Haustür in das Vorhaus mit dem Kreuzgratgewölbe aus dem 16. Jahrhundert und in den rückwärtigen Innenhof (rechts). Die Luke rechts führt in den Keller, die Holzstiege links ins Obergeschoß.*

Above: *The large dining table in the ground-floor living room is surrounded by old office chairs. The table is covered by a cloth woven in the traditional "ikat" style of Sumatra and under the window is the famous one-legged Stefan Wewerka "Einschwinger No. B5".*
Right: *seen from the front door, the entrance hall with its 16th-century cross-vaulting and a door leading to the inner courtyard (right). The hatch on the right gives access to the cellar, while the wooden staircase on the left leads to the upper floor.*

Ci-dessus: *la table de la salle à manger, au rez-de-chaussée. Les sièges sont de vieilles chaises de bureau; sur la table, un «ikat», étoffe traditionelle de Sumatra; sous la fenêtre, un exemplaire de la fameuse chaise asymétrique «Einschwinger No. B5» de Stefan Wewerka.*
A droite: *le vestibule, avec ses voûtes d'arête du 16e siècle, et la cour intérieure (au fond, à droite), vus depuis la porte d'entrée de la maison. La trappe, sur la droite, donne accès à la cave, et le petit escalier en bois, sur la gauche, à l'étage supérieur.*

Vorhergehende Doppelseite: Eine alte Zwillingstür trennt den Wohnraum im Erdgeschoß von Küche (links) und Speisekammer (rechts). Das Kreuzgratgewölbe stammt aus dem 16. Jahrhundert. Auf dem unbehandelten Fichtenholz-Boden liegen Strohmatten aus Mexiko. Die Möbel stammen aus den zwanziger, dreißiger, vierziger und fünfziger Jahren. Vor dem Ofen aus Gußeisen steht ein von Bruno Paul entworfener Sessel.

Rechts: Auf Nachttisch und Fensterbank im Gästezimmer stehen alte Vasen aus buntgesprenkeltem Überfangglas, Kerzenleuchter und eine kleine Chromleuchte aus den dreißiger Jahren.

Unten: das blaue Gästezimmer. Das alte Metallbett stammt von einem lokalen Trödler, der Eisenstuhl von einem Pariser Flohmarkt. Die Schaustellerfigur ist das Geschenk eines Hausgastes.

Previous pages: Antique twin doors separate the ground-floor living room from the kitchen (left) and the pantry (right). The cross-vaulting dates from the 16th century; Mexican straw matting covers the untreated spruce floor. The room is furnished with pieces from the Twenties, Thirties, Forties and Fifties, notably a Bruno Paul armchair set in front of the iron stove.

Right: On the bedside table and window sill in the guest room are antique vases of colourfully speckled cased glass, candlesticks and a small Thirties' chromium lamp.

Below: the blue guest room. The old iron bedstead came from a local junk dealer and the wrought iron chair from a Paris flea market. The display figure in the corner was a present from a house guest.

Double page précédente: Au rez-de-chaussée, une porte jumelée sépare le séjour de la cuisine (à gauche) et de l'office (à droite). La voûte d'arête remonte au 16e siècle; des nattes de paille du Mexique recouvrent en partie le sol en épicéa naturel. Le mobilier éclectique date des années vingt, trente, quarante et cinquante: devant le poêle en fonte, par exemple, un fauteuil de Bruno Paul.

Ci-dessus: sur la table de nuit et le rebord de la fenêtre, de vieux vases en verre doublé multicolore, des chandeliers et une petite lampe chromée des années trente.

Ci-dessous: la chambre d'amis ou «chambre bleue». Le vieux lit en métal a été déniché chez un brocanteur du coin, la chaise en fer, dans un marché aux puces parisien. Le personnage de fête foraine a été offert par un invité.

Oben: *das große Gästezimmer mit Messingbetten. Die unifarbenen Fleckerlteppiche sind eigens für diesen Raum angefertigt worden. Auf den Betten liegen amerikanische »Candystripe«-Wolldecken. Hinten links steht ein Lloyd-Loom-Stuhl, an der Wand rechts ein ehemaliger Werkstattisch und zwischen den Betten ein alter Metall-Waschtisch mit »Grasl«-Leuchten von Ingo Maurer.*
Rechts: *Steinfensterbank in der Speisekammer mit selbstgeschnitzten Steinschleudern, gefundenem Vogelnest und Keramiken.*

Above: *the large guest room with brass bedsteads. The monochrome rag rug was custom-made for the room. On the beds are American candy-striped woollen blankets. In the left-hand corner is a Lloyd Loom chair, and, against the wall on the right is a former work bench. A "Grasl" lamp by Ingo Maurer stands on an old metal washstand between the beds.*
Right: *the stone window sill in the pantry with hand-made catapults, a bird's nest and ceramics.*

Ci-dessus: *la grande chambre d'amis, avec ses lits en laiton. Les tapis en rapiéçages bariolés ont été confectionnés spécialement pour cette pièce; sur les lits, des couvertures en laine américaines à rayures multicolores. Au fond de la chambre, à gauche, un fauteuil Lloyd-Loom; contre le mur à droite, un ancien établi; entre les lits, une vieille table de toilette en métal, avec des lampes «Grasl» de Ingo Maurer.*
A droite: *sur le rebord en pierre de la fenêtre de l'office, des céramiques, un nid abandonné et des frondes de fabrication personnelle.*

For 50 years the 17th-century wooden shepherds' huts lay abandoned in one of the most primeval landscapes of Val Ferret, at 1 600 metres above sea level under the Mont Blanc massif. Then Glorianda Cipolla Vecchi rediscovered her inheritance. With her husband, the architect Andrea Vecchi, she converted these five "Baita", as they are called, into one large one. Here, the couple now spend idyllic summer days together with grandmother and two children. It is a well-established tradition that, whenever family circumstances change, so too does the house. The Vecchis, however, were fascinated by the possibility of restoring these old huts, which have been in the family for centuries, as faithfully as possible to the original. For this reason, they decided to dispense with all mod cons – there is no electricity, no fridge, and sometimes wolves come foraging for food left outdoors to cool in the night air.

Glorianda und Andrea Vecchi

Die im 17. Jahrhundert gezimmerten Schäferhütten, die »baita« genannt werden, liegen in einer der ursprünglichsten Landschaften, im Val Ferret auf 1 600 Meter Höhe unterhalb des Mont-Blanc-Massivs. 50 Jahre lang waren sie unbewohnt, bis Glorianda Cipolla Vecchi ihr Erbe neu entdeckte. Gemeinsam mit ihrem Mann, dem Architekten Andrea Vecchi, baute sie die fünf Hütten um, so daß eine größere »baita« entstand. In dieser verbringen sie nun samt Großmutter und zwei Kindern die schönsten Sommertage. Einer guten alten Tradition zufolge wurde das Haus umgebaut, wann immer sich die Familie veränderte. Die Vecchis waren fasziniert von der Möglichkeit, etwas konsequent Authentisches neu zu gestalten – jedes auch noch so kleine Teil ist seit Jahrhunderten im Familienbesitz – und verzichteten auf jeglichen modernen Komfort. So gibt es keinen Strom, keinen Kühlschrank. Und manchmal kommen nachts die Wölfe, um nach Speisen zu suchen, die zum Kühlen draußen gelagert werden.

Pendant 50 ans, les cabanes de bergers ou «baita», du val Ferret ont somnolé au milieu d'un paysage intact, situé à 1 600 mètres d'altitude, dans le massif du Mont-Blanc. Mais un jour, Glorianda Cipolla Vecchi redécouvre la propriété familiale construite au 17e siècle. Avec l'aide de son mari, l'architecte Andrea Vecchi, elle modifie les cinq bâtiments existants pour en faire une «baita» plus grande. Elle y passe maintenant les plus belles journées d'été avec grand-mère et enfants. La maison, ainsi le veut la tradition, se transforme aussi avec la famille. Les Vecchi, fascinés à l'idée de pouvoir créer du nouveau à partir de l'ancien tout en préservant le caractère profondément authentique des lieux (chaque élément est propriété de la famille depuis des siècles), ont renoncé à tout confort: ils n'ont ni électricité ni réfrigérateur. Alors, la nuit, parfois, les loups viennent chercher les restes de repas que la famille entrepose dehors pour les maintenir au frais.

Well away from the cosmopolitan social scene of St Moritz, on the Via Dimlej high above the lake, an enchanting house stands on the edge of the woods. The idyllic log cabin on its white plinth is a synthesis of the arts, created by the Swiss painter Mili Weber, who lived and worked here from the time the house was built in 1917, until her death in 1978. As you enter the house, where every last detail is perfectly thought out, you are plunged into a wonderful, fairy-tale world. Every corner, every niche, every cupboard was lovingly painted by the artist herself, who worked in the fresco style. Chubby-cheeked flower children, mythical creatures, water-sprites and fairies dance on the walls. Branches laden with berries entwine themselves around the furniture. Birds, fish, dragonflies and butterflies seem to hover about the house. Each is a testimony to Mili Weber's great love for the whole of creation. Today, the house where visitors can see most of the life's work of Mili Weber and her half-sister Anna Haller, is administered and meticulously preserved by a trust.

Mili Weber

Abseits vom mondänen Treiben der internationalen Society steht oberhalb des St. Moritzer Sees an der Via Dimlej ein märchenhaftes Anwesen am Waldesrand. Das kleine verwunschene Blockhaus auf weißem Mauersockel ist ein Gesamtkunstwerk, geschaffen von der Schweizer Malerin Mili Weber, die hier seit seiner Erbauung bis zu ihrem Tod 1978 lebte und arbeitete. Wenn man das bis ins kleinste Detail perfekt durchdachte Haus betritt, taucht man ein in eine wundersame Fabelwelt. Jede Ecke, jede Nische, jeden Schrank und jedes Kästchen hat die Künstlerin im Laufe ihres Lebens liebevoll »al fresco« bemalt. Pausbackige Blumenkinder und fröhliche Fabelwesen, Nixen und Feen tanzen an den Wänden, beerenbehangene Zweige ranken sich über die Möbel; Vögel, Fische, Libellen und Schmetterlinge scheinen durch das Haus zu schweben. Jedes Wesen legt Zeugnis ab von Mili Webers großer Liebe zur Kreatur. Heute wird das Haus, in dem ein Großteil des Lebenswerks von Mili Weber und ihrer Schwester Anna Haller zu besichtigen ist, von einer Stiftung liebevoll erhalten und verwaltet.

A la lisière d'une forêt, au-dessus du lac de Saint-Moritz, sur la Via Dimlej, se trouve une maison de conte de fées. C'est là, à l'abri de la vie mondaine et internationale de la station, que vécut jusqu'à sa mort, en 1978, le peintre suisse Mili Weber. La maison est une cabane en rondins posée sur un socle blanc, une véritable œuvre d'art qu'elle a parfaite au fil des ans. Passé la porte, on a l'impression d'être plongé dans un monde merveilleux. Pas un coin, niche, armoire ou coffret que l'artiste n'ait peint «al fresco». Sur les murs dansent des bambins joufflus et fleuris, des créatures fabuleuses, des fées, des ondines pleines de grâce et de jovialité. Des branches couvertes de baies grimpent le long des meubles. Mille poissons, oiseaux, libellules et papillons semblent nager ou virevolter dans la maison. Chaque créature porte témoignage de l'amour profond de Mili Weber pour la nature. On peut visiter la maison où est exposée une bonne partie de l'œuvre de Mili Weber et de sa sœur Anna Haller. C'est maintenant une fondation qui s'occupe de sa conservation et de son administration.

Alpen Interieurs   Mili Weber

Eingangsseiten, links: Mili Weber mit dem zahmen Rehli Fin; Außenansicht des Hauses, das 1917 von ihrem Bruder Emil erbaut wurde.
Eingangsseiten, rechts: das Treppenhaus. Links ein mit Märchenfiguren und Blumen bemalter Schrank. An der Wand hängen Gemälde von Mili Weber und Anna Haller.
Vorhergehende Doppelseite: das »Schloßzimmer«. Die Deckenmalerei zeigt die vier Jahreszeiten. Links erkennt man das reich bemalte große Puppenhaus, das »Schloß«, um deren Bewohner sich Mili Webers in neun Bänden festgehaltene Geschichten ranken. Rechts steht ein weiteres Puppenhaus vor Aquarellen mit »Blumenseelchen«, den von ihr geschaffenen Blumenkinder-Figuren.
Linke Seite: Blick aus dem »rosaroten Salon« ins »Schloßzimmer«. An den Wänden hängen Phantasieporträts von den Bewohnern des Puppenhauses. Die geschnitzte Holzdecke stammt von Emil Weber.
Oben: die Küche. Auf dem Tisch liegt das vorbereitete Futter für die Rehe, Hirsche, Eichhörnchen und Vögel, die sich im Winter ständig in der Umgebung des Hauses aufhielten und Mili Weber gegenüber zahm waren.

First pages, left: Mili Weber with her beloved pet deer, Rehli Fin; view of the outside of the house, built in 1917 by her brother Emil.
First pages, right: the stairs. On the left, a cupboard painted with flowers and fairy-tale characters. Hanging on the wall are paintings by Mili Weber and Anna Haller.
Previous pages: the "Castle Room". The frescoes on the ceiling represent the four seasons. On the left, we see the huge richly painted dolls' house, the "castle". Mili Weber wrote nine volumes of stories which revolved around the characters living in this "castle". On the right is another dolls' house, and behind it, a series of watercolours of Mili Weber flower-children characters.

Facing page: view from the "Pink Drawing Room" into the "Schloßzimmer" or "Castle Room". On the walls are "portraits" of the imaginary residents of the dolls' house. The carved wood ceiling is the work of Mili's brother Emil.
Above: the kitchen. On the kitchen table lies food prepared for the stags, roe deer, squirrels and birds which made their home each winter in the woods and fields surrounding the house and were tame in the presence of Mili Weber.

Première double page, à gauche: Mili Weber en compagnie de Rehli Fin, son chevreuil apprivoisé; vue extérieure de la maison construite en 1917 par le frère de l'artiste, Emil Weber.
Première double page, à droite: l'escalier avec son armoire encastrée et son plafond ornementé de poutres artistiquement peintes. Au mur sont accrochées des peintures de Mili Weber et Anna Haller.
Double page précédente: la «pièce du château». Les peintures du plafond représentent les quatre saisons. Sur la gauche, on reconnaît la grande maison de poupée, le «château», que Mili Weber a peinte avec art et autour de laquelle elle a tissé une histoire en neuf volumes. A droite se trouve également une maison de poupée, devant des aquarelles représentant les «petites âmes fleurs», les figures d'enfants-fleurs créées par l'artiste.
Page de gauche: vue du «salon rose» depuis la «pièce du château» ou «Schloßzimmer». Au mur sont accrochés des portraits pleins de fantaisie des habitants de la maison de poupée. Emil Weber a réalisé le plafond sculpté.
Ci-dessus: la cuisine. Sur la table, on aperçoit la nourriture préparée pour les chevreuils, les cerfs, les écureuils et les oiseaux. En hiver, ils ne s'éloignaient pas des environs de la maison et se montraient très dociles envers Mili Weber.

Rechts: *Die von Mili Weber mit Blumen und Vögeln bemalte Hausorgel umgibt ein Fresko mit Engelschören. Das Instrument mit zwei Manualen und 350 Pfeifen stammt aus der Werkstatt der Orgelbaufirma Metzler in Felsberg. Mili Weber spielte gut und gern, besonders Werke von Johann Sebastian Bach. Sie selbst komponierte ein Oratorium für Gesang, Violine und Orgel.*
Unten: *der Arbeitsplatz der Künstlerin. Rechts ein vollendetes Gemälde, links hinten ein Selbstporträt im Alter von 20 Jahren und ein Selbstbildnis, das während ihrer Münchner Studienzeit zwischen 1912 und 1914 entstand.*

Right: *The house organ, decorated by Mili Weber with painted flowers and birds, and surrounded by frescoes of angel choirs, has two manuals and 350 pipes. It was built at the Metzler workshop in Felsberg. Mili Weber was a skilled organist and particularly enjoyed playing the works of Johann Sebastian Bach. She herself composed an oratorio for chorus, violins and organ.*
Below: *the artist's studio. On the right, a finished painting; in the background on the left, two self-portraits: one at the age of twenty, the other painted between 1912–14 when she was studying in Munich.*

A droite: *L'orgue doté de deux claviers et de 350 tuyaux provient de l'atelier Metzler de Felsberg. Mili Weber l'a décoré de fleurs et d'oiseaux et l'entouré d'une fresque de chœurs d'anges. L'artiste, bonne musicienne, aimait beaucoup jouer, en particulier des œuvres de Jean-Sébastien Bach. Elle composa même un oratorio pour violons et orgue.*
Ci-dessous: *l'atelier de l'artiste. A droite, un tableau achevé. A gauche, au fond, un autoportrait de Mili à 20 ans et un autre autoportrait réalisé pendant ses études à Munich, en 1912–1914.*

Oben: *das Gästezimmer mit Erker. Hier befinden sich Werke von Mili Weber und befreundeten Künstlerinnen und Künstlern. Unter dem Fenster stehen Skulpturen von Milis Bruder Otto (1880–1912), einem bekannten Bildhauer seiner Zeit, der ihr das Kunststudium in München ermöglichte.*
Rechts: *ein Detail der bemalten Decke im »Bärenzimmer«.*

Above: *the guest room with oriel window. The room contains works by Mili Weber and her artist friends. Beneath the window are sculptures by Mili Weber's brother Otto (1880–1912), a well-known sculptor of his day, who enabled his sister to study art in Munich.*
Right: *detail of the painted ceiling of the "Bear Room".*

Ci-dessus: *la chambre d'amis avec une partie en saillie. On y trouve des œuvres de Mili Weber et d'amis artistes. Sous la fenêtre, des sculptures du frère de Mili, Otto (1880–1912), un sculpteur connu en son temps et qui aida sa sœur à faire ses études aux Beaux-Arts.*
A droite: *un détail de la «pièce aux ours».*

As a child, Dr Hermann Wirthner, father of the present occupant of Ammern hamlet lived here in extreme poverty, scratching a living as a goatherd. Money provided by the local priest enabled Dr Wirthner, who died in 1996, to study medicine. In the Fifties, he and his wife Rosemarie, a psychologist and teacher, were able to start to buy and restore the sixteen crumbling buildings that made up the tiny village in the Valais. Today, his daughter Karolin, a restorer and conservationist, lives here with her partner Helmut Kiechler, a veterinary technician and craftsman. The preservation of Ammern (the name derives from "Amoltren", meaning "wild cherries") has become their life's work. To do justice to this mammoth task, they have opened the village to visitors, whose guided tour ends with a congenial aperitif. Anyone who falls in love with Ammern can come back at any time. One of the houses can be rented as a holiday home.

Karolin Wirthner

Der Vater der heutigen Bewohnerin des Weilers Ammern hat hier in seiner Kindheit als Ziegenhirte in ärmsten Verhältnissen gelebt. Ein Stipendium des Pfarrers ermöglichte dem 1996 verstorbenen Dr. Hermann Wirthner sein Medizinstudium. Mit seiner Frau Rosemarie, einer Psychologin und Lehrerin, konnte er seit den fünfziger Jahren das vom Verfall bedrohte, aus 16 Gebäuden bestehende Dörfchen im Wallis erwerben und retten. Heute lebt dort seine Tochter Karolin, Restauratorin und Konservatorin, mit ihrem Lebensgefährten Helmut Kiechler, Tierpräparator und Handwerker. Den Erhalt von Ammern – abgeleitet von »Amoltren« (Wilde Kirschen) – haben sie sich zur Lebensaufgabe erkoren. Um dieser großen Herausforderung gerecht werden zu können, haben sie ihr Dorf für Besucher geöffnet. Die Dorfführung endet mit einem gemütlichen Aperitif. Wer sich in Ammern verliebt hat, darf wiederkommen. Ein Gebäude wird als Ferienhaus vermietet.

Le père de l'actuelle propriétaire du hameau de Ammern, le docteur Hermann Wirthner, décédé en 1996, fut chevrier dans son enfance et vécut dans la plus grande misère, mais grâce au soutien financier du prêtre de la paroisse il put faire des études de médecine. Avec sa femme Rosemarie, psychologue et professeur, il acheta dans les années cinquante ce hameau valaisan constitué de seize bâtisses et le sauva ainsi de la ruine. Leur fille Karolin, restaurateur et conservateur, y vit aujourd'hui avec son compagnon Helmut Kiechler qui est taxidermiste et artisan. Tous deux consacrent leur vie à la sauvegarde de Ammern (nom dérivé du mot «Amoltren» qui signifie «cerises sauvages»). Pour venir à bout de cette tâche, ils ont ouvert le hameau au public. La visite des lieux s'achève sur un apéritif convivial. Tout visiteur qui tombe amoureux de Ammern peut y revenir et louer une des maisons pour y passer des vacances.

Alpen Interieurs   Karolin Wirthner

Alpen Interieurs   Karolin Wirthner

Eingangsseiten: Ansicht des Weilers Noversch im Tal von Gressoney, Aostatal.
Vorhergehende Doppelseite, links: Blick auf das 1640 erbaute Haupthaus des Weilers Ammern und die Walliser Alpen; ein geschmückter Widderschädel; die sanft im Wind klingenden Glöckchen sollen irdische und unirdische Geister von dem Dörfchen fernhalten.
Vorhergehende Doppelseite, rechts: Die Häuser des Weilers sind aus unbehandeltem Lärchenholz gebaut, das im Laufe der Jahrhunderte von der Sonne angebrannt ist.
Linke Seite: die Eingangstür zum zweiten Wohnhaus aus dem 18. Jahrhundert, das auch als Ferienhaus vermietet wird.
Oben: Die Steinplatte trennt Vorratsspeicher und Unterbau. Im Hintergrund rechts eine Brotleiter und links eine Waldsäge.
Rechts: winterliches Stilleben.

First pages: view of the hamlet of Noversch in the Gressoney Valley, Valle d'Aosta.
Previous pages, left: A view of the main house built in 1640 in the hamlet of Ammern in the Valais Alps; a ram's skull decorated with foliage; tinkling softly in the wind, the bells are said to deter earthly and unearthly spirits from invading the small village.
Previous pages, right: The houses in the hamlet are built of untreated larch wood, burnt over the centuries by the sun.
Facing page: the front door of the second house, built in the 18th century and now rented out as a holiday home.
Above: The stone slab separates the storeroom from the cellar. In the background, a bread ladder on the right and a woodcutter's saw on the left.
Right: wintry still-life.

Première double page: le hameau de Noversch dans la vallée de Gressoney, Val d'Aoste.
Double page précédente, à gauche: vue sur la maison principale du hameau, construite en 1640, et sur les Alpes valaisanes; un crâne de bélier décoré de feuillages; les clochettes qui tintent doucement au vent sont censées éloigner les esprits d'ici-bas et de l'au-delà.
Double page précédente, à droite: Les maisons sont construites en bois de mélèze non traité, brûlé par le soleil au cours des siècles.
Page de gauche: la porte d'entrée de la deuxième maison, bâtie au 18e siècle et louée aux vacanciers.
Ci-dessus: Une dalle isole le grenier à provisions du soubassement. A l'arrière-plan, sur la droite, une échelle pour monter le pain et, sur la gauche, une scie à bois.
A droite: nature morte hivernale.

Oben: *Die Wohnstube dient gleichzeitig als Aufenthalts-, Schlaf- und Arbeitsraum. Tisch und Truhe stammen aus dem 18. Jahrhundert, die Stühle aus der Zeit des Biedermeier und des Jugendstil. Die Teppiche sind aus Stoffresten gewebt.*
Rechts: *Das mäusesichere Vorratsschränkchen wird heute für Geschirr genutzt. Die alten Stiche zeigen »Das Stufenalter des Mannes«, von der Geburt bis zum Tod.*
Rechte Seite: *Auf dem Küchentisch aus dem 18. Jahrhundert hat die Hausherrin eine Bauernmahlzeit gerichtet. An der Wand hängt das Hauskruzifix.*

Above: *The main room serves as living room, bedroom and workshop. The table and chest are 18th-century, the chairs are Biedermeier and Art Nouveau, the rugs are woven from scraps of cloth.*
Right: *a mouse-proof store cupboard, now used for crockery. The antique engravings show "The Ages of Man", from birth to the grave.*
Facing page: *The mistress of the house has served a peasant-style meal on the 18th-century kitchen table. On the wall is a crucifix.*

Ci-dessus: *Le séjour sert à la fois de salon, de chambre à coucher et de pièce de travail. La table et le coffre datent du 18e siècle, les chaises sont de styles Biedermeier et Art nouveau, et les tapis ont été réalisés avec des restes de tissus.*
A droite: *un petit garde-manger hors de portée des souris, affecté aujourd'hui au rangement de la vaisselle. Les vieilles gravures représentent les divers âges de la vie de l'homme.*
Page de droite: *sur la table de la cuisine datant du 18e siècle, un repas campagnard préparé par la maîtresse de maison. Un crucifix est accroché au mur.*

Rechts: *eine Anrichte aus dem 18. Jahrhundert mit Büchern.*
Unten: *Die Balken des doppelten Etagenbettes sind alte, vor dem Verfall gerettete »Tillbäume« aus dem Nachbardorf. Auf diesen Tragbalken hinterließen die Erbauer und Besitzer des Hauses das Erbauungsjahr und fromme Sprüche. Rechts im Foto ist ein Specksteinofen zu sehen, der Schafwollteppich ist handgewebt.*

Right: *18th-century dresser with books of the same period.*
Below: *The supports of the bunk beds were originally "Tillbäume", beams rescued from the neighbouring village on which the names of the builders and owners of the house are carved, along with pious inscriptions. On the right is a soapstone stove; the sheep's wool rug is hand-woven.*

A droite: *un bahut et des livres du 18e siècle.*
Ci-dessous: *Les montants des lits superposés sont taillés dans de vieux «Tillbäume», de vieilles poutres maîtresses, provenant de maisons du village voisin et sauvées à temps de la dégradation. Y sont gravés le nom du constructeur et du propriétaire, l'année de construction et des formules pieuses. Sur la droite, se trouve un poêle en stéatite; le tapis en laine de mouton a été tissé à la main.*

Oben: Das Unterbett wurde früher zum Schlafen herausgezogen. So bot die Kammer Platz für sechs bis sieben Personen.
Rechts: Der Specksteinofen in der Stube wird von der Küche aus befeuert. Die Stubentür weist handgearbeitete Intarsien aus Nußbaum- und Lindenholz auf. Die weißen Halterungen am Kinderbett dienten der »Fesselung« des Babys, wenn die Eltern auf dem Feld arbeiteten.

Above: The spare bed used to be pulled out from under the bunk, to providing sleeping accommodation for six to seven people.
Right: The soapstone stove in the "Stube", or living room, is heated from the kitchen. The living room door has hand-carved marquetry panels in walnut and lime wood. The white supports on the cot were used to tether the baby while the parents were working in the fields.

Ci-dessus: Le lit de dessous était autrefois tiré le soir, permettant ainsi d'accueillir six à sept personnes.
A droite: Le poêle en stéatite du séjour est chauffé depuis la cuisine. La porte du séjour est décorée d'une marqueterie en noyer et en tilleul. Les points d'attache blancs du petit lit servaient à maintenir l'enfant en place pendant que les parents étaient aux champs.

Oben: in der Alphütte. In dem einfachen Aufenthaltsraum der Alp-
knechte sieht man an der Wand Löffel aus Holz und Aluminium. Auf
zwölf Quadratmetern lebten hier früher vier Knechte.
Rechts: Im Wohnraum des Haupthauses steht der Auferstehungs-
christus, eine einheimische, geschnitzte, farbig gefaßte und vergoldete
Holzskulptur aus dem 18. Jahrhundert. Vorne eine Laterne.
Rechte Seite: in der Mühle. Im Vordergrund stehen vor einem Sack
mit gemahlenem Korn »Fischeln« zum Messen des Getreides.

Above: inside the alpine hut. Once a very modest home to farm
labourers, four men used to live in a space of twelve square metres.
On the wall are wooden and aluminium tablespoons.
Right: In the living room of the main house is a gilded and painted
wooden statue of the Risen Christ, carved by a local craftsman back
in the 18th century. In the foreground is a hurricane lamp.
Facing page: in the mill with "Fischeln", grain measures; in the foreground and a sack of ground corn behind.

Ci-dessus: l'intérieur du chalet d'alpage. Cette pièce simple de douze
mètres carrés hébergeait autrefois quatre vachers. Sur le mur, des
cuillères en bois et en aluminium.
A droite: Le «Christ ressuscité», statuette datant du 18e siècle, se
trouve dans la salle de séjour du bâtiment principal; cette sculpture
montée sur un socle est en bois peint et doré. Au premier plan, une
lanterne.
Page de droite: le moulin. Au premier plan, des mesures à grains
dites «Fischeln»; derrière, un sac de céréales moulues.

Alpen Interieurs   Karolin Wirthner

The neoclassical manor house may look a little incongruous amid the magnificent Upper Bavarian landscape. The austere, white façade shines out across the windswept meadows, through the mighty oaks and luxuriant chestnut trees lining the drive. Professor of architecture Roderich Fick was 43 years old and had travelled halfway around the world, from Greenland to Cameroon, when he built the house in 1929. Furnishing the house with its balanced proportions posed no problems for journalist and author Sibylle Zehle, whose work includes visiting and writing about dream hotels from Bali to Capri and from Paris to Patagonia. "I simply mix everything together, the dignified with the witty, the exquisite with the exotic, the rustic with the artistic. It only takes a little imagination to furnish a home where anything goes."

Sibylle Zehle

Fast wirkt das strenge neoklassizistische Herrenhaus ein wenig fremd inmitten der üppigen oberbayerischen Landschaft. Klar und schlicht leuchtet die weiße Fassade zwischen wogenden Wiesen, wuchtigen Eichen und imposanten Kastanien am Weg. Der Architekturprofessor Roderich Fick war 43 Jahre alt, als er das Anwesen im bayerischen Fünfseengebiet im Jahre 1929 erbaute, und hatte bereits die halbe Welt bereist – von Grönland bis Kamerun. Der Journalistin und Autorin Sibylle Zehle, die beruflich unter anderem die schönsten Traumhotels zwischen Bali und Capri, Paris und Patagonien besucht und beschrieben hat, fiel das Einrichten des Hauses mit den ausgewogenen Proportionen leicht: »Ich mische einfach alles, Würdiges und Witziges, Kostbares und Kurioses, Country und Kunst. Es gibt nichts Phantasieloseres als eine Wohnung, in der alles stimmt.«

Il semble presque déplacé, ce manoir néoclassique, dans la végétation exubérante de la Haute-Bavière. Aucune tourelle, aucun encorbellement pour le décorer, aucun pignon ou balcon en bois sculpté comme sur les chalets typiques. La sobre façade d'un blanc lumineux et sobre se détache sur le vert des prés ondoyants, des chênes vigoureux et des châtaigniers touffus. Le professeur d'architecture Roderich Fick avait 43 ans en 1929 lorsqu'il entreprit de construire cette maison dans la région bavaroise des Cinq lacs. Il connaissait déjà la moitié du monde, du Groenland au Cameroun. L'actuelle propriétaire Sibylle Zehle est journaliste et écrivain. Son travail consiste, entre autres, à visiter les plus beaux hôtels du monde, de Capri à Bali, de Paris à la Patagonie, et à en faire la description. Elle n'eut aucun mal à décorer le manoir en raison de ses belles proportions: «Je mélange tous les ingrédients, le respectable et l'amusant, le précieux et le curieux, le rustique et l'art. Rien n'est plus dénué de fantaisie qu'une maison où tout est parfait.»

Vorhergehende Doppelseite, links: Das von Roderich Fick 1929 erbaute Haus ist denkmalgeschützt und wird heute von der Autorin Sibylle Zehle und ihrem Mann, einem Manager, bewohnt.

Vorhergehende Doppelseite, rechts: Über süddeutschem Biedermeier hängt »Winterabend am Blankeneser Süllberg«, ein Gemälde von Eduard Bargheer (1901–1979), einem der bedeutendsten Künstler der Hamburgischen Sezession.

Oben und rechts: Stilmix im lichtdurchfluteten Wohnzimmer: Country und Kunst. Alle Böden im Haus sind aus kanadischem Pitchpine-Holz.

Rechte Seite: Zwischen den Türen, die hinaus auf eine Steinterrasse führen, ein Biedermeier-Sessel aus Wien von 1807. Darüber hängt eine Papierzeichnung von Walter Dahn aus dem Jahre 1987.

Previous pages, left: The house is now the home of author Sibylle Zehle and her husband, a business executive; it was built in 1929 by Roderich Fick and is under a preservation order.

Previous pages, right: Hanging above an example of southern German Biedermeier is "Winter evening at Blankenese Süllberg", a painting by Eduard Bargheer (1901–1979), one of the leading members of the Hamburg Secession movement.

Above and right: a mixture of artistic and rustic styles in the light-flooded living room. The floors throughout the house are Canadian pitch pine.

Facing page: between the doors leading out onto a paved terrace, a Biedermeier armchair made in Vienna in 1807. Above it is a 1987 drawing by Walter Dahn.

Double page précédente, à gauche: La maison bâtie par Roderich Fick en 1929 est classée monument historique. Elle est habitée aujourd'hui par l'écrivain Sibylle Zehle et son mari, un directeur d'entreprise.

Double page précédente, à droite: au-dessus d'une table Biedermeier, un tableau d'Eduard Bargheer (1901–1979), «Soir d'hiver sur le Süllberg à Blankenese». Le peintre était un des artistes majeurs de la Sécession hambourgeoise.

Ci-dessus et ci-dessous: mélange de genres dans le salon inondé de lumière où voisinent style rustique et objets d'art. Tous les planchers de la maison sont en pitchpin canadien.

Page de droite: entre les portes-fenêtres qui s'ouvrent sur la terrasse en pierre, un fauteuil viennois de style Biedermeier de 1807. Au-dessus, se trouve un dessin sur papier de Walter Dahn datant de 1987.

Linke Seite: Die Bibliothek im ersten Stock ist das Herz des Hauses.
Oben links: Der Biedermeier-Schreibschrank von 1820 stammt aus
einem österreichischen Adelshaus, der Stuhl aus der Wiener Werkstatt
Josef Danhausers (1820–1840).
Oben rechts: Die Photoarbeit »It could be Elvis« ist von der amerika-
nischen Künstlerin Louise Lawler.

Facing page: The library on the first floor is the heart of the house.
Above left: The 1820 Biedermeier writing desk with cupboards came
from an Austrian stately home, the chair from the Viennese workshop
of Josef Danhauser (1820–1840).
Above right: The photomontage "It could be Elvis" is by the American artist Louise Lawler.

Page de gauche: La bibliothèque située au premier étage est le cœur
de la maison.
Ci-dessus, à gauche: Le secrétaire Biedermeier qui date de 1820 provient d'un château autrichien, la chaise, de l'atelier de l'ébéniste viennois Joseph Danhauser (1820–1840).
Ci-dessus, à droite: «It could be Elvis», œuvre photographique de
l'Américaine Louise Lawler.

In 1948, while still a student of architecture, Pierre Zoelly carried out the first renovation of the Villa Mappina, his family's country house, built in the Tessin region of Switzerland in 1622. 45 years later and by now an internationally esteemed architect, he was obliged to do it all over again. The Villa Mappina had burnt to the ground. Zoelly took a courageous step. "The more deeply attached to tradition I feel", he says, "the more deliberately modern I can be." The low, flat-roofed extension of steel, concrete and glass adjoining the old villa is constructed of prefabricated sections, industrial sheet metal, T-beams and aluminium casing of the type used in the aerospace industry. Zoelly calls it "a dialogue between technology and history". The sixteen-metre swimming pool also serves as a reservoir and hence protection against fire. Against the backdrop of rocky mountain scenery, the pool, like the extension, looks almost transparent and at one with the rugged, exotically lush countryside.

Pierre Zoelly

1948 baute Pierre Zoelly, der damals noch Architekturstudent war, das erste Mal die Familienvilla Mappina um. 45 Jahre später und mittlerweile zu einem international angesehenen Architekten avanciert, mußte er es noch einmal tun. Denn die Villa, ein Tessiner Landhaus aus dem Jahre 1622, war bis auf die Grundmauern niedergebrannt. Zoelly wagte einen mutigen Schritt. »Je mehr ich mich der Tradition verhaftet fühle«, sagt er, »um so bewußter kann ich modern sein«. Der flache Villenanbau aus Stahl, Beton und Glas besteht aus vorgefertigten Bauteilen, Industrieblechen, T-Trägern und Aluminiumverkleidungen aus der Flugzeugindustrie und ist für Zoelly ein »Dialog von Technik und Geschichte«. Der 16 Meter lange Swimmingpool dient gleichzeitig als Wasserreservoir, also als Brandschutz. Parallel zum felsigen Berg gebaut, wirkt er – genauso wie der Anbau – transparent und leicht, so daß er mit der ebenso rauhen wie exotisch wuchernden Natur fast eine Einheit bildet.

La Villa Mappina, maison de campagne construite dans le Tessin en 1622, appartient depuis longtemps à la famille Zoelly. C'est en 1948 que Pierre Zoelly, alors étudiant en architecture, transforma la maison pour la première fois. 45 ans plus tard, il fallut la reconstruire, la villa ayant été détruite par un incendie. L'architecte connu qu'il était devenu entre-temps se lança à cette époque dans une entreprise architectonique hardie. «Plus je me sens lié à la tradition, plus je peux être sciemment moderne», affirme-t-il. Il a reconstruit l'ancienne villa en la complétant par une aile au toit plat, tout en acier, béton et verre. Pour ce bâtiment annexe, il a adopté des solutions résolument modernes: composants préfabriqués, tôles industrielles, poutres métalliques en forme de T et revêtements en aluminium utilisés dans l'industrie aéronautique. Zoelly voit dans cette réalisation un «dialogue entre la technique et l'histoire». La piscine de 16 mètres de long fait aussi office de réservoir d'eau en cas d'incendie. Contruite parallèlement à la montagne rocheuse, elle paraît presque transparente, à l'instar de l'annexe, et comme intégrée à la nature sauvage et luxuriante.

Vorhergehende Doppelseite, links: *die ockerfarbene Villa Mappina; der moderne Anbau wirkt beinahe transparent.*
Vorhergehende Doppelseite, rechts: *Vom Wohnzimmer aus schweift der Blick weit über den Zürichsee.*
Rechts und unten: *Der 16 Meter lange Pool aus Beton schließt sich wie eine Verlängerung an den flachen Anbau an.*

Previous pages, left: *Beside the ochre-coloured villa, the modern extension appears almost transparent.*
Previous pages, right: *From the living room, the view extends far across Lake Zürich.*
Right and below: *Sixteen metres long, the concrete swimming pool appears to be a continuation of the low, flat-roofed extension.*

Double page précédente; à gauche: *la villa avec sa façade ocrée; l'annexe, par son architecture moderne, donne l'impression d'être presque transparente.*
Double page précédente, à droite: *Le salon offre un vaste panorama sur le lac Zurich.*
A droite et ci-dessous: *La piscine en béton semble être un prolongement naturel de l'annexe.*

Die Wand aus Stahlträgern und Industrieblech stößt unvermittelt auf
die sechzig Zentimeter dicken Mauern von 1622. Große Schiebe-
fenster und -türen mit Aluminiumrahmen öffnen sich zur Landschaft.

The wall of steel beams and industrial sheet metal immediately ad-
joins the sixty-centimetre-thick walls built in 1622. Large sliding aluminium windows and doors open onto the rocky hillside.

La paroi de l'annexe, avec ses poutres en acier et sa tôle industrielle,
prolonge directement les murs de 60 centimètres d'épaisseur
construits en 1622. De grandes fenêtres et portes coulissantes s'ouvrent
sur le paysage.

Linke Seite: Der pavillonähnliche Anbau bietet einen Panoramablick
auf See und Berge. Ein quadratischer Tisch dient als Eß- oder Arbeitsplatz. Die schlichten Bugholzstühle sind bunt gestrichen.
Oben: Blick vom Schlafzimmer in den felsigen Garten.

Facing page: The pavilion-like extension provides an all-round view of
the lake and mountains. The rectangular table is used for both dining
and working. The simple bentwood chairs are brightly painted.
Above: view from the bedroom into the rocky garden.

Page de gauche: L'aile en forme de pavillon offre une vue panora-
mique sur le lac et les montagnes. La grande table rectangulaire sert
à la fois de coin repas et de bureau. Les chaises en bois cintré, toutes
simples, ont été peintes dans des tons vifs.
Ci-dessus: vue de la chambre à coucher donnant sur le jardin
rocailleux.

Oben und links: *Das Bootshaus diente dem Bildhauer Kaspar von Zumbusch bis zu seinem Tod im Jahre 1915 als Atelier.*
Rechte Seite: *in der Morgensonne: Dr. Caspar und Annemarie von Zumbusch; ihr Haus Essbaum.*

Above and left: *The sculptor Kaspar von Zumbusch used the boat house as a studio until his death in 1915.*
Facing page: *Dr. Caspar and Annemarie von Zumbusch enjoy the morning sunshine; their house, Essbaum.*

Ci-dessus et à gauche: *Le hangar à bateaux a servi d'atelier au sculpteur Kaspar von Zumbusch jusqu'à sa mort en 1915.*
Page de droite: *sous le soleil matinal, Caspar et Annemarie von Zumbusch; leur maison Essbaum.*

Alpen Interieurs   Annemarie und Caspar von Zumbusch

As you look out from Haus Essbaum – the word means "fenced field for horses" – across the Chiemsee, you feel you could almost touch the mountains. For 13 years, Dr. Caspar von Zumbusch, retired lawyer and banker, and his wife Annemarie have lived in the house, built in the pre-industrial age at the beginning of the 18th century as a smallholding. In 1906, the present owner's grandfather Kaspar von Zumbusch (1830–1915), the sculptor whose best-known achievements include the Maria-Theresia Monument, one of the symbols of Vienna, bought the property as a summer residence, and commissioned Otto Riemerschmid to redesign it. There is a magnificent tiled stove in each of the many rooms, where the children and grandchildren love to come and stay. On the walls hang family portraits, painted by Ludwig von Zumbusch (1861–1927), son of the sculptor. The boat house with landing stage, where Kaspar von Zumbusch set up a small studio, is only a few steps away from the house.

Annemarie und Caspar von Zumbusch

Wenn der Blick von Haus Essbaum, was »eingezäunte Pferdeweide« bedeutet, über den Chiemsee geht, liegt die Bergkette zum Greifen nah. Dr. Caspar von Zumbusch, Jurist und Bankdirektor im Ruhestand, und seine Frau Annemarie leben seit 13 Jahren hier. Ihr Haus wurde in vorindustrieller Zeit zu Beginn des 18. Jahrhunderts als Kleinbauernanwesen erbaut. Der Großvater, der Bildhauer Kaspar von Zumbusch (1830–1915), der unter anderem das berühmte monumentale Maria-Theresia-Denkmal, ein Wahrzeichen Wiens, schuf, erwarb das Anwesen 1906 als Sommerhaus und ließ es von Otto Riemerschmid umbauen. In jedem der vielen Zimmer – Kinder und Enkel kommen gern zu Besuch – stehen prachtvolle Keramiköfen. An den Wänden hängen Familienporträts, die Ludwig von Zumbusch (1861–1927), Sohn des Bildhauers, malte. Das Boots-haus mit Badesteg, in dem Kaspar von Zumbusch sich ein kleines Atelier eingerichtet hatte, liegt nur wenige Schritte entfernt.

Lorsque le regard se porte sur le lac de Chiemsee depuis la propriété de Essbaum (le «clos aux chevaux»), la chaîne de montagnes semble être à portée de main. Caspar von Zumbusch, juriste et directeur de banque en retraite, et sa femme Annemarie vivent là depuis 13 ans, dans une maison de petits fermiers construite au début du 18e siècle. Le grand-père, le sculpteur Kaspar von Zumbusch (1830–1915) auquel on doit, entre autres, le monument à la mémoire de l'impératrice Marie-Thérèse, un des emblèmes de Vienne, acheta la propriété en 1906 et la fit transformer par l'architecte Otto Riemerschmid pour l'utiliser comme résidence d'été. Les nombreux pièces de la maison (les enfants et les petits-enfants viennent volontiers en visite) sont toutes dotées de poêles de faïence magnifiques. Aux murs sont accrochés des portraits de famille peints par le fils du sculpteur, Ludwig von Zumbusch (1861–1927). Le hangar aux bateaux, qui servait d'atelier à Kaspar von Zumbusch, et son ponton se trouvent à quelques mètres seulement de la maison.

Oben: *Die Truhen in der Diele im ersten Obergeschoß stammen aus dem 18. und 19. Jahrhundert.*
Rechts: *Die Deckenbemalung stammt von Leo von Zumbusch, dem Vater des jetzigen Hausbesitzers.*
Rechte Seite: *Im ehemaligen Kuhstall befindet sich seit der Jahrhundertwende das Speisezimmer. Gegessen wird gern am blanken Holztisch.*

Above: *The chests in the first-floor hallway date from the 18th and 19th centuries.*
Right: *ceiling painting by Leo von Zumbusch, father of the actual owner.*
Facing page: *The former cowshed has been used as a dining room since the turn of the century. It is a pleasure to eat at the bare wooden table.*

Ci-dessus: *Les coffres du vestibule, au premier étage, datent du 18e et du 19e siècle.*
A droite: *La peinture du plafond est de Leo von Zumbusch, le père du propriétaire actuel.*
Page de droite: *L'ancienne étable a été transformée au début du siècle en salle à manger. La famille prend volontiers ses repas sur la table de bois nue.*

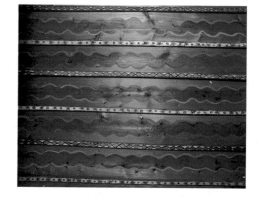

Oben: *Die Stellfläche aus Ziegelsteinen diente früher als »Milch-bank«. Heute werden hier Vorräte aller Art gelagert.*
Rechte Seite: *Die frühere Remise dient heute als Küche. Auf dem mit Holz befeuerten Emaille-Herd wird bei großen Familienfeiern noch immer gekocht.*

Above: *Once used to keep milk cool, the brick-built pantry is now used for general storage.*
Facing page: *A former outbuilding is now the kitchen. The old wood-burning enamel stove is still used occasionally to cook for big family celebrations.*

Ci-dessus: *Dans le buffet en briques qui était utilisé jadis comme «dépôt de lait», sont entreposées aujourd'hui toutes sortes de provi-sions.*
Page de droite: *l'ancienne remise transformée en cuisine. Le vieux fourneau à bois en émail sert encore à cuisiner, à l'occasion de grandes fêtes familiales.*

Oben links: *der Bildhauer Kaspar von Zumbusch und seine Frau bei der Goldenen Hochzeit, von ihrem Sohn Ludwig von Zumbusch gemalt.*
Oben rechts: *ein Porträt des elfjährigen Leo von Zumbusch, gemalt von seinem Bruder, dem Maler Ludwig von Zumbusch.*
Rechte Seite: *Den prachtvollen Keramikofen baute der Hafner Klampfleuthner, dessen Familie auf der Fraueninsel im Chiemsee in der achten Generation Öfen brennt.*

Above left: *the sculptor Kaspar von Zumbusch and his wife painted by their son Ludwig to commemorate their golden wedding anniversary.*
Above right: *a portrait of Leo von Zumbusch at the age of eleven, painted by his brother, the painter Ludwig von Zumbusch.*
Facing page: *a magnificent tiled stove, built by Klampfleuthner whose family has been manufacturing stoves on the Fraueninsel, an island on the Chiemsee, for eight generations.*

Ci-dessus, à gauche: *un portrait du sculpteur Kaspar von Zumbusch et de sa femme réalisé par leur fils Ludwig à l'occasion de leurs noces d'or.*
Ci-dessus, à droite: *un portrait de Leo à l'âge de onze ans, peint par son frère, le peintre Ludwig von Zumbusch.*
Page de droite: *un magnifique poêle de faïence de Klampfleuthner, appartenant à une famille d'artisans qui fabrique, depuis huit générations, des poêles en carreaux glacés sur l'île de Fraueninsel («île aux Dames»), située sur le Chiemsee.*

Appenzeller Volkskundemuseum
CH–9063 Stein AR

Gebrauchsgegenstände aus dem Sennerleben, Trachten, Schmuck und Möbel, gewebte und gestickte Textilien sind in diesem Museum versammelt.

The Appenzell Folk Museum houses dairy farming equipment, traditional costumes, jewellery and furniture, weaving and embroidery.

Le Musée des arts et traditions populaires de l'Appenzell illustre la vie sur l'alpe, avec objets utilitaires, costumes folkloriques, bijoux, meubles, tissage et broderie.

Freilichtmuseum Ballenberg
CH–3855 Brienz

Rund 80 historische Wohn- und Handwerkshäuser aus der gesamten Schweiz wurden in dem Museum im Berner Oberland wieder aufgebaut.

Around 80 historic houses and workshops have been brought from all over Switzerland and reconstructed in the Ballenberg Open Air Museum in the Bernese Oberland.

Exposition historique d'environ 80 habitations et ateliers originaires de toute la Suisse présentée à l'Ecomusée Ballenberg dans l'Oberland bernois.

Holzknechtmuseum
Laubau 12
D–83324 Ruhpolding

Auf einem großen Freigelände mit Hütten erfährt man alles über das Alltagsleben der Holzknechte.

Large open air museum with huts and everything related to the daily life of woodcutters.

Tout sur la vie quotidienne des bûcherons, présentée dans son milieu naturel avec les cabanes traditionnelles.

Schloß Juval
I–39020 Kastelbell/Castelbello
(Seite/Page 142–149)

Reinhold Messner zeigt in seinem Museum Skulpturen aus Tibet und Indien, Bilder zum Thema »Yeti« und eine Sammlung zur 3 000 Jahre während Geschichte von Hinduismus, Buddhismus und Christentum.

Reinhold Messner presents Tibetan and Indian sculptures, pictures on the theme of the Yeti and a collection representing 3 000 years of Hindu, Buddhist and Christian symbolism.

Dans le château de Juval, Reinhold Messner expose des sculptures du Tibet et de l'Inde, des photos sur le «yéti» et une collection d'objets retraçant 3 000 ans de symbolique hindouiste, bouddhique et chrétienne.

Heimatmuseum Nutli Hüschi
Monbieler Straße
CH–7250 Klosters
(Seite/Page 176–181)

In einem 400 Jahre alten Originalhaus ist das bäuerliche Leben dargestellt. Ausgestellt werden Bauernmöbel, Hausrat, Werkzeuge.

Museum of rural life in an authentic 400-year-old house. Rustic furniture, household goods and tools.

Le Musée régional présente la vie paysanne dans son cadre original, un chalet de 400 ans. Meubles campagnards, ustensiles de ménage, outils.

Schloß Hellbrunn
A–5020 Salzburg

In dem weitläufigen Park des frühbarocken Lustschlosses befinden sich Grotten, Weiher und die weltberühmten Wasserspiele. Im Monatsschlößl ist das Salzburger Volkskundemuseum untergebracht.

Early baroque summer residence with extensive parkland, grottos, ponds and the world-famous fountains. Salzburg folklore is housed in the nearby Monatsschlößl.

Château de plaisance des débuts du baroque, avec son vaste parc, ses grottes, ses étangs et ses fameux jeux d'eau. Le Monatsschlößl abrite le musée des arts et traditions populaires salzbourgeois.

Heimatmuseum Schliersee
Lautererstraße 6
D–83727 Schliersee

In einem Bauernhaus aus dem 15. Jahrhundert werden Zeugnisse bäuerlicher Wohnkultur, Trachten und Werkzeuge vom 17. bis 20. Jahrhundert gezeigt.

Exhibits illustrating rural life, traditional costumes and implements dating from the 17th to the 20th century, displayed in a 15th-century farmhouse in the Schliersee Local History Museum.

Le Musée régional de Schliersee présente dans une ferme du 15e siècle des témoignages de l'habitat, de l'outillage et des costumes régionaux du 17e au 20e siècle.

Museum für Alltagskultur
I–39044 Neumarkt/Egna

Dieses Museum bietet einen guten Einblick in die lokale Alltagskultur des 19. Jahrhunderts. Die Ausstellungsbandbreite reicht von Schulzeugnissen über Postkarten bis zu Möbeln, Spielzeug und Handwerksgerät.

The Museum of Everyday Life in South Tyrol offers an insight into everyday life in the 19th century, with everything from school reports and postcards to furniture, toys and tools.

Le Musée de la vie quotidienne au Tyrol du Sud offre le tour d'horizon de l'habitat et de la vie dans la région au 19e siècle, du mobilier et du jouet à l'outillage, jusqu'au bulletin scolaire et à la carte postale.

Danksagung / Acknowledgements / Remerciements

Dieses Buch widme ich dem Kunsthändler Konrad Otto Bernheimer, München, London, Montevideo, dessen Familie die deutsche Kultur geprägt hat und deren Lebensweg – Emigration im Dritten Reich, Rückkehr und erneuter Erfolg der Nachkriegsgeneration – mir Inspiration und Mahnung zugleich ist. Auf seiner Burg Marquartstein, die in diesem Buch zum ersten Mal veröffentlicht ist, haben Bernheimer und seine Frau Barbara versammelt, was fünf Generationen wichtig war: Buddha-Statuen und Kunstschätze der Medici mit Blick auf das weite bayerische Land und die Berge. Kinderlachen und der Duft von frischgebackenem Kuchen sind das Zeugnis von Hier und Heute. Mein Dank geht an Dr. Angelika Taschen, die diese Buch-Reihe herausgibt, und an den Verleger Benedikt Taschen, junge Leute mit Visionen, eine seltene Spezies im Verlagsgeschäft.

Beate Wedekind

I dedicate this book to the art dealer Konrad Otto Bernheimer of Munich, London and Montevideo, whose family has left its mark on German culture and whose journey through life – a tale of emigration in the Third Reich, their return home and the renewed success of the postwar generation – is both an inspiration and a reminder to me. In his fortress of Marquartstein, the secrets of which are revealed for the first time in this book, Bernheimer and his wife Barbara have brought together family heirlooms spanning five generations – Buddha statues and art treasures of the Medici, all overlooking the broad expanse of the Bavarian countryside and its mountains. It is a place full of children's laughter and the smell of freshly-baked cakes, a place of life and vitality. My thanks go to Dr. Angelika Taschen, editor of this book series, and to the publisher Benedikt Taschen. These young people of vision are a rare species in the world of publishing today.

Beate Wedekind

Je dédie ce livre au marchand d'art Konrad Otto Bernheimer, Munich, Londres, Montevideo. Sa famille a marqué la culture allemande de son empreinte, et sa vie – émigration sous le IIIème Reich, retour et nouvelle réussite de la génération d'après-guerre – est pour moi à la fois objet de réflexion et d'inspiration. Dans son château de Marquartstein, présenté pour la première fois dans cet ouvrage, Bernheimer et son épouse Barbara ont rassemblé les trésors familiaux d'hier – Bouddha et les trésors artistiques des Médicis avec vue sur le vaste paysage bavarois et les Alpes – et d'aujourd'hui – les rires d'enfants et l'odeur des gâteaux sortant du four. Je tiens à remercier Dr. Angelika Taschen, responsable de cette collection, et l'éditeur Benedikt Taschen, des personnes jeunes qui ont une conception claire de leurs objectifs, ce qui est rare dans ce métier.

Beate Wedekind

Adressen / Addresses / Adresses

Konrad Otto Bernheimer
Promenadeplatz 13
D–80333 München

Alexander Mayerhofer
Salzburger Blumenstube
Universitätsplatz 14
A–5020 Salzburg

Galerie Thaddaeus Ropac
Villa Kast
Mirabellplatz 2
A–5020 Salzburg

Palazzo Salis
Piazza Salis 3
I–23037 Tirano (SO)

Segantini Museum
Via Somplaz 30
CH–7500 St. Moritz
(ab Juli 1999)

Jocelyne und Jean-Louis Sibuet
Les Fermes de Marie
Chemin de la Riante Colline
F–74120 Megève

Mili Weber-Stiftung
Via Dimlej 35
CH–7500 St. Moritz

Karolin Wirthner
Freilichtmuseum
Ammern
CH–3981 Blitzingen